EEN491-Heroes of the Women's Suffrage Movement (eBook)

Enslow Publishers 6 Volumes Flipbook
Set Price: $335.46
Reading Level: 6th Grade
Interest Level: Middle
Accelerated Reader: No

This series introduces teen readers to the courageous and fiery pioneers of the women's rights movement. These are women who fought against long odds and often violent opposition to gain all women, indeed all persons, the equality, dignity, and civil and human rights that today we frequently take for granted. Though there is still a long way to go down the road to true equality of the sexes, these biographies allow readers to celebrate the women who have carried us so far and provisioned us so well.

Title	Code	List Price	Our Price	Copyright	Prg
Champions for Women's Rights: Matilda Joslyn Gage, Julia Ward Howe, Lucretia Mott, and Lucy Stone	EEN078857	$74.55	$55.91	2017	
Elizabeth Blackwell: Doctor and Advocate for Women in Medicine	EEN078840	$74.55	$55.91	2017	
Elizabeth Cady Stanton: Founder of the Women's Suffrage Movement	EEN078833	$74.55	$55.91	2017	
Sojourner Truth: Women's Rights Activist and Abolitionist	EEN078819	$74.55	$55.91	2017	
Susan B. Anthony: Social Reformer and Feminist	EEN078826	$74.55	$55.91	2017	
The Seneca Falls Convention: Working to Expand Women's Rights	EEN078864	$74.55	$55.91	2017	

THE SENECA FALLS CONVENTION

WORKING TO EXPAND WOMEN'S RIGHTS

 DEBORAH KENT

 Enslow Publishing

101 W. 23rd Street
Suite 240
New York, NY 10011
USA

enslow.com

Published in 2017 by Enslow Publishing, LLC.
101 W. 23rd Street, Suite 240, New York, NY 10011

Library of Congress Cataloging-in-Publication Data

Names: Kent, Deborah, author.
Title: The Seneca Falls convention : working to expand women's rights / Deborah Kent.
Description: New York : Enslow Publishing, 2017. | Series: Heroes of the women's suffrage movement |
Audience: Grade 9 to 12. | Includes bibliographical references and index.
Identifiers: LCCN 2016001037 | ISBN 9780766078925 (library bound)
Subjects: LCSH: Women's rights—United States—Juvenile literature. | Women—United States—Social
conditions—Juvenile literature. | Feminism—United States—History—Juvenile literature.
Classification: LCC HQ1236.5.U6 K45 2016 | DDC 305.40973—dc23
LC record available at http://lccn.loc.gov/2016001037

Printed in the United States of America

To Our Readers: We have done our best to make sure all websites in this book were active and
appropriate when we went to press. However, the author and the publisher have no control over and
assume no liability for the material available on those websites or on any websites they may link to. Any
comments or suggestions can be sent by e-mail to customerservice@enslow.com.

Photo Credits: Cover, pp. 18, 23, 28, 35, 59, 68, 80–81, 94, 97 Library of Congress; cover, interior
design elements: wongwean/Shutterstock.com (grunge background on introduction, back cover);
Attitude/Shutterstock.com (purple background); Sarunyu_foto/Shutterstock.com (white paper roll);
Dragana Jokmanovic/Shutterstock.com (gold background); Eky Studio/Shutterstock.com (grunge back-
ground with stripe pattern); macknimal/Shutterstock.com (water color like cloud); Borders-Kmannn/
Shutterstock.com (vintage decorative ornament); pp. 9, 38 Hulton Archive/Getty Images; p. 11 Peter
Stackpole/Time Life Pictures/Getty Images; p. 13 DEA Picture Library/Getty Images; p. 30 United
States Mint/File:Abigail Adams First Spouse Coin reverse.jpg/Wikimedia Commons; p. 37 Anti-Slavery
Society, including Lucretia Mott (b/w photo), American Photographer, (19th century)/Schlesinger
Library, Radcliffe Institute, Harvard University/Bridgeman Images; p. 40 Archive Photos/Getty Images;
pp. 48, 51, 53, 57, 111 National Park Service; p. 61 Universal History Archive/Getty Images; p. 70
Suffragette Demonstration in London, from 'Le Petit Journal', 1908 (coloured engraving), French School,
(20th century)/Private Collection/Archives Charmet/Bridgeman Images; p. 72 Print Collector/Getty
Images; p. 76 Portrait of Elizabeth Cady Stanton (1815-1902) and Susan B. Anthony (1820-1906),
c.1880 (b/w photo), American Photographer, (19th century)/Schlesinger Library, Radcliffe Institute,
Harvard University/Bridgeman Images; p. 79 National Archives and Records Administration/File:Petition
of E. Cady Stanton, Susan B. Anthony, Lucy Stone, and others (1865).jpg/Wikimedia Commons; p.
86 Women suffragists picketing in front of the White House, Washington DC, pub. 1917 (b/w photo),
American Photographer, (20th century)/Private Collection/The Stapleton Collection/Bridgeman
Images; p. 88 Stock Montage/Getty Images; p. 99 Harold M. Lambert/Getty Images; p. 103 David
Fenton/Getty Images.

CONTENTS

"HARD IS THE FORTUNE"

The women and men who came from England to the 13 American colonies brought a wealth of folklore and traditions to the New World. They carried their religious beliefs, their remedies for common ailments, and the folktales and songs that were their entertainment on long winter nights. One song that made its way to North America is known as "The Wagoner's Lad." It has been found in many versions and locations. It tells the story of a girl who must give up her beloved because her father does not approve of him. The first stanza runs,

> Hard is the fortune of all womankind:
> She's always controlled, she's always confined;
> Controlled by her father until she's a wife,
> Then a slave to her husband all the rest of her life.[1]

The stories of countless generations of women are embodied in the words of this simple song. Women in early America had little control over their own lives. Social custom and a series of laws enforced the idea that women belonged in the home. An unmarried woman was under the control of her father or other male relatives. When a woman married, she essentially became her husband's charge. She could not make any decision about money or property. Men were thought to be responsible adults, while women were treated as helpless children.

Most of the laws in the colonies, and later in the young United States, were based upon the laws of England. In 1765 a British legal scholar named William Blackstone wrote, "The very being or legal existence of the woman is suspended during the marriage."[2] In other words, a married woman had so little power that she did not exist as a separate person under the law.

As early as the 1700s, however, some women in England and the United States began to protest their condition. A few wrote books on the subject, and others gave public lectures. As time passed, isolated protesters found one another. They began to discuss their grievances and exchange ideas about what could be done.

Little by little, women ceased to be passive sufferers submitting quietly to their fate. In the summer of 1848 a group of women and men gathered in Seneca Falls, New York, to share their ideas about women's rights. They approved a series of 11 resolutions that pointed the way toward change. One of those resolutions, the most controversial of all, declared that women should have the right to vote.

It is not easy to change patterns that have been entrenched for hundreds, even thousands, of years. Women worked for decades to secure their rights as equal members of society. Throughout the long struggle they looked back at the Seneca Falls Convention as a major turning point. The gathering in Seneca Falls launched a movement that transformed the world.

CHAPTER ONE

A TEA PARTY AND A TURNING POINT

In the spring of 1848 James and Lucretia Mott set out on a long journey from their home in Philadelphia. The Motts were dedicated abolitionists, people who worked to end the institution of slavery. Crowds flocked to hear Lucretia Mott speak about slavery and its evils. She was known as a passionate fighter for justice.

THE WOMAN ON THE PLATFORM

Only a few years earlier, it would have been unthinkable for a woman to speak publicly to an audience mixed with men and women. Then, in the 1830s, a few brave women uprooted the notion that they could not and should not speak publicly to men. Lucretia Mott was among the first women in the United States to break down the restrictions on female lecturers.

By 1848 Mott was among the most popular public speakers in the United States. She lectured on temperance (the restricted use of alcohol), the evils of slavery, prison reform, and the rights of women. Some people attended her lectures to argue and jeer, but many others went to listen and be inspired.

The Motts belonged to a religious group called the Society of Friends, or Quakers. Quakers believed that all human beings are equal in the sight of God. Many Quakers believed that it was morally wrong for one group of human beings to enslave another. For this reason, a number of abolitionists came from a Quaker background.

In a speech to the American Anti-Slavery Society in New York City, Lucretia Mott expressed a spirit of optimism. She pointed out that the abolition movement had gained considerable momentum over the past 15 years, evidence that society was progressing toward a new age of freedom. "Go on," she urged her listeners, "and make advancement by our faithfulness."[1]

Leaving New York City, the Motts headed to the Cattaraugus Indian Reservation near the city of Buffalo. The Ogden Land Company had pressured the Seneca Nation, part of the Haudenosaunee, or Iroquois, Confederation, to sell large tracts of reservation land. The Motts and other Quakers intervened and worked to ensure that the Seneca could stay on their reservation. During her 1848

Lucretia Mott was one of the masterminds behind the Seneca Falls Convention, the first convention devoted to women's rights in the United States.

Lucretia Mott

visit, Lucretia Mott observed the schools on the reservation and noted that the Seneca were making progress.

From Cattaraugus, Lucretia Mott and her husband traveled into Canada. Near Toronto they visited a colony of African Americans who had been enslaved in the United States. Because they had managed to escape across the border, these women and men were now free and safe from recapture. In the *Liberator*, a major antislavery

LUCRETIA MOTT, THE FIGHTING QUAKER

Lucretia Coffin Mott (1793–1880) dedicated her life to fighting for the abolition of slavery, the rights of women, and prison reform. She grew up in a Quaker family in Massachusetts and moved to Philadelphia with her husband, James Mott. Lucretia Mott became a Quaker minister and, despite opposition from conservative branches of the church, began to lecture on abolition and women's rights. In 1838, she and other antislavery activists were threatened by a mob. Ten years later, Mott was among the women who organized the Seneca Falls Convention on women's rights. Following the Civil War, she did her best to heal divisions that developed in the movement for women's suffrage. She also was a committed pacifist and worked to end war and violence.

newspaper, Lucretia Mott wrote joyfully, "The spirit of Freedom is arousing the world."[2]

Early in July, the Motts headed to the town of Auburn, New York, where they stayed with Lucretia's younger sister, Martha Coffin Wright. Martha was eager to introduce her sister to some of her Quaker friends in the surrounding communities. On July 9 the two women were invited for tea at the home of Jane and Richard Hunt in the nearby town of Waterloo. Lucretia would

Members of women's temperance unions crusaded against alcohol consumption, often in local bar rooms. These groups also spoke out against slavery and championed women's rights.

meet a number of active Quaker women, including Martha's friend Mary Ann M'Clintock. Furthermore, an old friend of Lucretia's would be there, a woman she had met on a trip to London eight years before. Lucretia Mott was eager to reconnect with Elizabeth Cady Stanton.

THE WOMEN BEHIND THE CURTAIN

Lucretia Mott and Elizabeth Cady Stanton met in London at an international antislavery convention. Stanton's husband, Henry, was a delegate to the convention. Most of the delegates were men, but several female delegates attended as well. Lucretia Mott was among them.

Before the convention proceedings began, many of the male delegates expressed their outrage that women would take an active part. They claimed that women belonged in the home and should leave public affairs to men. As the debate grew more heated, men quoted passages from the Bible to support their arguments. Many years later, Elizabeth Cady Stanton wrote, "It was really pitiful to hear narrow-minded bigots, pretending to be teachers and leaders of men, so cruelly remanding their own mothers, with the rest of womankind, to absolute subjection to the ordinary masculine type of humanity."[3]

The debate about women's participation in the convention stretched over several days. At last, a

Lucretia Mott and Elizabeth Cady Stanton first met in 1840 at the World Anti-Slavery Convention, held in Exeter Hall from June 12 to June 23. Although the delegates were to be solely men, some women were admitted.

vote decided that the female delegates would not be permitted to vote or even to speak. Furthermore, all of the women present must sit in a separate section of the meeting room, "curtained off like a choir." A handful of the male delegates, including the abolitionist William Lloyd Garrison, chose to support the women by sitting with them behind the curtain. "After battling so many long years for the liberties of African slaves," Garrison declared, "I can take no part in a convention that strikes down the most sacred rights of all women."[4]

For Stanton, the antislavery convention was a bitter disappointment. She described the convention sessions as "twelve of the longest days in June." However, her spare time was brightened by her deepening acquaintance with the female delegates, and with Lucretia Mott in particular. "As we walked about to see the sights of London, I embraced every opportunity to talk with her," she wrote later. "It was intensely gratifying to hear all that, through years of doubt, I had dimly thought, so freely discussed by other women."[5] Mott introduced Stanton to the writings of a British woman named Mary Wollstonecraft, who published a book called *A Vindication of the Rights of Woman* in 1792.

In the years to come, Stanton contended that her meeting with Lucretia Mott planted the seed of a radical idea. "We resolved to hold a convention as soon as we returned home," she wrote in her autobiography, "and form a society to advocate the rights of women."[6] However, Mott's writings do not support Stanton's story. In her diary, Mott described Stanton as "bright, open, [and] lovely," and commented, "I love her now as one belonging to us."[7] Yet Mott made no reference to plans for a women's rights convention. Though she was a passionate advocate for women's rights, she was chiefly focused on the abolition of slavery while she was in London.

When Mott and Stanton returned to the United States, any ideas about a women's rights convention were set aside. Mott continued with her travels and her lectures. Stanton was soon occupied with the day-to-day business of running a home and caring for small children.

MARY WOLLSTONECRAFT, VINDICATING THE RIGHTS OF WOMAN

Mary Wollstonecraft (1759–1797) grew up in a suburb of London. Her father squandered the family's fortune and was often abusive. As a young woman, Wollstonecraft operated a school and worked as a live-in governess. While she struggled to support herself, she thought about society's unequal treatment of women and men.

In 1792, she wrote a ground-breaking book called *A Vindication of the Rights of Woman*. She concluded that education was the key to women's opportunity. She called for women to receive the same education that was provided to men.

During her lifetime, Wollstonecraft was harshly criticized for her radical views. However, women's rights leaders such as Lucretia Mott recognized her as a trailblazer. Today, *A Vindication of the Rights of Woman* is considered one of the earliest works of the women's rights movement.

ELIZABETH CADY STANTON

Elizabeth Cady was born to a well-to-do family in Johnstown, New York, in 1815. Her father, Daniel Cady, was a lawyer and a judge. As a child, Elizabeth often listened when neighbors consulted Judge Cady about their legal problems.

One day, a woman named Flora Campbell arrived in great distress. She explained that her father had died and left her a valuable farm. Without Flora's permission, her husband had mortgaged the property. Now, creditors threatened to drive the family from their home.

Elizabeth felt sure that her father could solve Flora Campbell's problem. To her dismay, however, he explained that she had no right to the property she had inherited. Under the law, all of a wife's property belonged to her husband. Judge Cady could do nothing to help Flora Campbell.

Elizabeth never forgot Flora Campbell and the many other women who brought their legal troubles to the judge. Over and over, she saw that the laws of the land kept women subservient to men. She vowed to do what she could to help women stand beside men as equals.

Elizabeth Cady married the abolitionist Henry Stanton in 1840. In a break with tradition, she decided to keep her maiden name and add her husband's surname, becoming Elizabeth Cady Stanton.

In 1847 Elizabeth Cady Stanton moved with her husband and their three small boys to the town of Seneca Falls, New York. A number of abolitionists and other social reformers lived in the area, but she was so busy she had little time to make their acquaintance. Henry Stanton was often away for weeks on end, and all the responsibility for maintaining the household rested on Elizabeth's shoulders. "To keep a house and grounds in good order, purchase every article for daily use, keep the wardrobes of half a dozen human beings in proper trim, take the children to dentists, shoemakers, and different schools, or find teachers at home, altogether made sufficient work to keep one brain busy," she wrote in her autobiography.[8]

The Stantons lived on the outskirts of town, and many of their neighbors were immigrants from Ireland. They were poor people with little education, and many of the men drank heavily. Sometimes neighbor women called on Stanton to settle family disputes, and from time to time she was summoned late at night to help deliver a baby. Her own life was hard, but she came to see that the lives of women in poverty were far more difficult.

AT TEA IN WATERLOO

For two months, the Stanton children and the household servants had been grievously ill with malaria. Nursing the sick day and night, Elizabeth

This monument to the pioneers of the women's suffrage movement celebrates Elizabeth Cady Stanton, Susan B. Anthony, and Lucretia Mott. The monument is on permanent display at the US Capitol.

Cady Stanton worked until she was exhausted. In her autobiography she reflected, "The general discontent I felt with woman's portion as wife, mother, housekeeper, physician, and spiritual guide, the chaotic conditions into which everything fell without her constant supervision, and the wearied, anxious look of the majority of women impressed me with a strong feeling that some active measures should be taken to remedy the wrongs of society in general, and of women in particular."[9]

Stanton was thrilled by the prospect of an afternoon tea. It would provide her with the chance to get to know some of the reform-minded Quakers who lived in the area, and she could reconnect with Lucretia Mott. She lived in a state of "mental hunger," and this gathering was the food she needed.

Richard P. Hunt was a wealthy wool merchant. Shawls from his woolen mills in Seneca Falls were sold all over the country. He had chosen to manu-facture woolen products rather than products made from cotton in order to avoid using materials pro-duced by slave labor.

The Hunts lived in a large brick house on the eastern edge of Waterloo. The tea was held in the parlor, a comfortable room with a red velvet sofa, two rocking chairs, and a large rug on the floor. In the center of the room stood a big square table with a marble top, where Jane Hunt had set out her best teacups and saucers.[10]

In this group of women, Stanton was an out-sider. All of the others were Quakers, and most of them came from Philadelphia. Jane Hunt and most of her guests expected to spend the afternoon talking about dissension in their local Quaker meeting. Instead, they found them-selves listening to the pent-up frustrations of the stranger from Seneca Falls. "I poured out, that day, the torrent of my long-accumulating discon-tent," Stanton wrote later, "with such vehemence and indignation that I stirred myself, as well as the rest of the party, to do and dare anything."[11]

Stanton's outburst unleashed a tide of sympathy. Soon the other women were sharing their own frustrations and grievances. According to a story handed down in the Hunt family, Richard Hunt stepped into the parlor and overheard the women's conversation. After he listened for a few moments, he asked, "Why don't you do something about it?"[12]

The women agreed that they would. Sitting around the marble-topped table in the Hunts' parlor, they decided to hold a convention on the rights of women.

CHAPTER TWO

BEGINNING WITH EVE

"**W**ell-behaved women seldom make history,"[1] writes the social historian Laurel Thatcher Ulrich. Ulrich meant that, unless a woman broke the rules laid down by society, she lived in obscurity. Her name and life were quickly forgotten. Tradition supported the belief that God intended women to be inferior to men. After all, according to the account in the book of Genesis, God made the first woman, Eve, from a rib of the first man, Adam.

The personal histories of few women who lived in early America have come down to us today. Most women lived quietly and obediently. They left few traces besides their marriage records and their headstones in the village churchyard.

To understand the revolution that began with the Seneca Falls Convention, it is important to examine the lives of women in the thirteen colonies and in the young republic that was formed after the American Revolution. Women lived under severe restrictions that Lucretia Mott, Elizabeth Cady Stanton, and other fighters for women's rights sought to overturn.

SPINNING, CHURNING, AND WAITING

A number of men in the 13 British colonies distinguished themselves as soldiers, political leaders, writers, painters, and inventors. But for the vast majority of colonial women, life centered around the home. If a woman lived on a farm, as most colonists did, her domain was a small house, its surrounding yards, a kitchen garden, and perhaps an orchard. She rose before dawn to begin the day's work—milking the cow, lighting the kitchen fire, and preparing the morning meal. Throughout the day she cared for the chickens and pigs, tended the garden, cooked meals, swept and scrubbed the floors, and sewed and mended her family's clothes. Most likely she had a number of children, perhaps as many as ten or twelve, all clamoring for her attention.

Slavery was practiced throughout the colonies. Life for enslaved African American women was far more difficult and restricted than life for women of European descent. The lives of enslaved women were not their own; they belonged to the master or mistress. The most cruel aspect of slavery was the destruction of families, as children were often sold away from their parents.

Most colonial-era women were bound to the home. They were responsible for all things connected to keeping the home and family running, with little to no thoughts of education or socialization outside their family.

The colonial farm woman made most of the things her family needed. She churned butter and made her own cheese, soap, and candles. Probably a spinning wheel stood in a corner of the main room of the house. The woman might earn a bit of money by spinning wool or flax into thread that she sold to the local weaver. Since all of her earnings belonged to her husband, he determined how her spinning money would be spent.

POETS OF THE COLONIES

Few colonial women had the chance to become famous. However, two of the best-known poets of early America were women: Anne Bradstreet and Phillis Wheatley.

Anne Bradstreet (1612–1672) grew up in a wealthy English family. Although she never went to school, she received an excellent education by studying the books in her father's extensive library. In 1630, she and her husband immigrated to colonial Massachusetts. Bradstreet endured the hardships of life in the wilderness, where she raised eight children. Her poems reflect her religious feelings and her pleasure in family life. Many of her poems were collected in *A Gentlewoman in New-England*, published in Boston in 1678.

Phillis Wheatley (1753?–1784) was born in West Africa and was sold into slavery when she was seven years old. She was purchased by the Wheatley family of Boston, and one of the Wheatley daughters taught her to read and write. When young Phillis began to write poetry, the Wheatleys nurtured her talent. Many of Phillis's poems dealt with religious themes or celebrated famous leaders, such as George Washington.

Some white colonists did not believe that a young African American woman was capable of writing serious poetry. In 1772, a group of learned Bostonians subjected Wheatley to a trial, questioning her at length about her knowledge of vocabulary, history, and classical literature. They were forced to conclude that she was indeed the author of the poems she claimed to have written. A collection of Wheatley's work appeared in *Poems on Various Subjects*, published in 1773.

As farmhouses were widely scattered, a visit from a sister or neighbor was a special treat, an occasion to be cherished. If a colonial woman lived in a town or city, she had the advantage of neighbors close by. Her world extended to the local market, where she bargained for produce and where she might sell eggs or baked goods. Like her country cousins, she worked long days at home, caring for her husband and children.

If a family had the means to send some of its children to school, usually the boys were the ones to receive an education. Girls, it was assumed, had no need for book learning. Since most colonial women were illiterate, few of them captured their day-to-day lives in letters or diaries. One of the exceptions was Mary Vial Holyoke of Salem, Massachusetts. Here are some of the entries in her diary from

1760: "Washed," "Ironed," "Scoured pewter," "Scoured furniture [and] brasses and put up the chintz bed and hung pictures," "Sowed peas," "Pulled first radishes," "Bought a pig to keep," "Preserved quinces. Made syrup of cores and parings," "Made two barrels of soap." As busy as she was, it's no wonder her entries were brief![2]

Life for men in the colonies was hard, too. Farmers did heavy, back-breaking work in the fields, haunted by worries about drought and crop failure. But at the end of the day a man could return home to rest, waited upon by his wife. Furthermore, a man had the freedom to travel away from home and to relax in the tavern.

Men were expected to take part in the affairs of the community. They served in the militia and on the village fire brigade and the local police force. In some colonies, especially in New England, they helped make decisions at town meetings. Men worked in many professions, all of which were closed to women. They became doctors, lawyers, merchants, and ministers. Their choices were limited only by their abilities, interests, and financial resources.

Women were expected to stay at home while men did the "important" work in life. Men went into the world, and women waited. Their role was to wait quietly, obediently, keeping the home ready for the men's return.

THE RULE OF LAW

Laws varied from one colony to another, but everywhere the impact on women was the same. A colonial husband had almost absolute authority over his wife. If she brought land or money into the marriage, it belonged to him from the moment she said, "I do." If she earned income, her husband owned all of her earnings. The marriage vows themselves enforced the husband's dominance. The bride had to promise that she would "love, honor, and obey" her future husband.

As William Blackstone put it, a married woman had no legal existence. In practical terms, this meant that she could not sign a contract or sue another party. Furthermore, she could not be held legally responsible for her actions if she went into debt or committed a crime. Her debts and her crimes were the responsibility of her husband.

Because men were held accountable for the behavior of their wives, it was in the husband's interest to keep his wife in line. Wife beating, or "domestic chastisement," was fully legal, as long as the wife's injuries were not too severe. According to Thomas Fuller, a seventeenth-century British clergyman, "A woman, a dog, and a walnut tree, The more you beat them, the better they be."[3]

Divorce was possible in colonial America, but it was very difficult to obtain. When divorce did occur, the wife was generally considered at fault. Her

COPYRIGHTED BY M. MARQUES, 1884.

THROUGH THE CONSTANT USE OF LIQUOR HE LOSES, AT TIMES, ALL CONTROL OF HIMSELF.
AND IN ONE OF THESE MOMENTS KILLS HIS WIFE.

JAN 26 1885

Domestic violence was an evil women simply had to endure if they intended to stay married. It was nearly impossible to leave a marriage, since women had no rights of their own, not even to their own children.

property went to her husband, and she was usually left destitute. If the couple had children, the husband gained custody. Because divorce was likely to be so disastrous, women rarely left even the unhappiest marriages.

Women had no way to change the laws that put them at such disadvantages. They could not speak at town meetings or other public gatherings, and they could not hold public office. They were forced to live by laws that they had no hand in making.

One group of women, however, lived by a very different code. The women of the Haudenosaunee, or Iroquois, of western New York and the upper Great Lakes region took an active role in the political life of the community. A Christian missionary who lived among the Haudenosaunee wrote, "The women were the great power among the clan, as everywhere else. They did not hesitate, when occasion required, to knock off the horns, as it was technically called, from the head of a chief and send him back to the ranks of the warriors. The original nomination of the chiefs also always rested with the women."[4]

Lucretia Mott visited the Seneca, a member nation of the Haudenosaunee, in 1848. Elizabeth Cady Stanton had met members of another Haudenosaunee nation, the Oneida, when she visited her cousin, the abolitionist Gerrit Smith. Some scholars suggest that their knowledge of the Haudenosaunee helped these women imagine a society in which women and men lived as equals.

"WHY EXCLUDE WOMEN?"

In 1776 the 13 American colonies hovered on the brink of war, ready to separate from Great Britain. At the First Continental Congress in Philadelphia, a group of colonial leaders hammered out plans for achieving independence. One of the strongest voices in the Continental Congress belonged to John Adams of Massachusetts.

While her husband was away in Philadelphia, Abigail Adams waited at their home in Braintree, Massachusetts, caring for their children. She and her husband wrote long letters back and forth. On March 31, 1776, in a letter that has become famous in the women's rights movement, Abigail Adams wrote, "[I]n the new code of laws which I suppose it will be necessary for you to make I desire you would remember the ladies. … Remember all men would be tyrants if they could. If particular care and attention is not paid to the ladies we are determined to foment a rebellion and will not hold ourselves bound by any laws in which we have no voice or representation."[5]

Future US first lady Abigail Adams was an early champion of women's rights, by way of her influential husband, founding father John Adams.

In his next letter, John Adams dismissed his wife's suggestion with a quip about "petticoat despotism." Nonetheless, she apparently set him thinking. He and the other Continental Congress leaders hoped to craft a democratic nation, its government based upon the consent of its people. Yet how could they claim to design a government of the people when women and African Americans had no part in making the laws? "Shall we say that every individual of the community, old and young, male and female, as well as rich and poor, must consent, expressly, to every act of legislation?" John Adams wrote to a friend. "Whence arises the right of the men to govern the women? ... Why exclude women?"[6]

The founders of the new United States could not accept the radical notion of a true democracy

THE NEW JERSEY EXPERIMENT

In 1776, lawmakers in New Jersey took the call for equal representation seriously regarding women. Women of property (most of them wealthy widows) were allowed to vote in state and national elections. Since only men of means were allowed to vote at that time, women and men were on an equal footing. In 1807 massive corruption in New Jersey elections led the legislature to reexamine the state's voting practices. Although women were not responsible for the widespread voting fraud, women's suffrage was revoked.

in which all people had the right to participate. The institution of slavery was kept alive, and women continued to be barred from voting or holding office. The old British laws that Blackstone wrote about in 1763 became embedded in the new legal system.

Yet every beginning brings with it a sense of hope. Here and there, women in the new republic imagined that change lay ahead. In 1790 a Massachusetts woman named Judith Sargent Murray wrote, "I expect to see our young women forming a new era in female history."[7] The time of waiting was drawing to a close. Soon would dawn a time for action.

CHAPTER THREE

THE AGE OF REFORM

In 1776, the Declaration of Independence stated that "all men are created equal, that they are endowed by their Creator with certain inalienable Rights, that among these are Life, Liberty and the pursuit of Happiness." The ideas expressed in this document reflect the influence of the English philosopher John Locke. Locke believed that all people are equal and independent. The French philosopher Jean-Jacques Rousseau also influenced thought in the early years of the United States. Rousseau believed that human beings are naturally free, good, and wise. Only the rules and expectations of society draw people away from their original state.

The ideas of Locke, Rousseau, and others led to an eighteenth-century philosophical movement called the Enlightenment. The Enlightenment encouraged science, education, and the questioning of long-held religious and political beliefs. In the United States, Enlightenment philosophy led to an era that is often called the Age of Reform.

THE ELM AND THE VINE

For most Americans in 1831, the idea of a woman speaking publicly to an audience of both men and women was unacceptable. For a woman to speak to an audience of white and African American men and women was more radical still. In 1831 an African American woman named Maria Stewart dared the impossible. She gave a series of lectures to a group of abolitionists in Boston, black and white, male and female. Four of Stewart's speeches were later published in *The Liberator*, a newspaper established by the abolitionist William Lloyd Garrison. "Possess the spirit of independence," Stewart urged African Americans. "You can but die if you make the attempt; and we shall certainly die if you do not."[1]

Two sisters from South Carolina, Sarah and Angelina Grimke, also helped break down the barriers for women in public speaking. Growing up in the South, the Grimkes witnessed the cruelty of slavery first hand. Their parents were slaveholders, as were most of their neighbors. When she was five years old, Sarah saw the brutal beating of an enslaved woman. From that day forward she fiercely opposed the captivity of her fellow human beings. Angelina grew to share her older sister's antislavery convictions.

In 1835, the Grimke sisters left the South. To the dismay of their family, they moved to Philadelphia and joined the growing movement for the abolition of slavery. With their personal stories of South Carolina, they were an invaluable asset to the antislavery cause.

At first, the Grimke sisters spoke only to women's antislavery groups. Then, in 1837, they began lecturing to audiences of both women and men. With the examples of Maria Stewart and the Grimke sisters before them, other women began to lecture publicly. Lucretia Mott, a passionate abolitionist, became the most famous female lecturer of her time.

Many people, especially the clergy, were outraged that women dared to speak out in public. One Congregational minister in Massachusetts wrote,

Sarah Grimke became an abolitionist after witnessing the horrors of slavery on her own family's plantation.

When [a woman] assumes the place and tone of man as a public reformer ... her character becomes unnatural. If the vine ... thinks to assume the independence and the overshadowing nature of the elm, it will not only cease to bear fruit, but fall in shame and dishonor into the dust.[2]

Some male abolitionists welcomed women's help in the cause. However, many objected to their full participation, pushing them to the sidelines. As a result, women began to form their own antislavery organizations. In 1833, a group of white and African American women, including Lucretia Mott and Sarah Mapps Douglas, established the Philadelphia Female Anti-Slavery Society. Another interracial group, the Boston Women's Anti-Slavery Society, was founded in the same year. These societies helped to educate the public about the evils of slavery. Since women could not vote, they used their right to petition to reach Congress with their message. They collected thousands of signatures and delivered the petitions to their representatives in Washington.

Thousands of reform-minded women in the United States also became active in the temperance movement. In the early nineteenth century, alcohol consumption was much higher than it is today. Drunken husbands often squandered family savings and were abusive toward their wives and children. Women led the way in advocating for

Lucretia Mott sits in the front row, second from right, in this 1851 photograph of the executive members of the Pennsylvania Anti-Slavery Society. Before this group admitted women, Mott helped establish a women's antislavery society.

temperance, or the moderate use of alcoholic beverages. Temperance organizations set up fountains in public places to provide clean drinking water as an alternative to alcoholic drinks. They opened "temperance coffeehouses" and "temperance theaters." They also pressed to establish "dry counties" where the sale of spirits was prohibited.

As was the case in the antislavery movement, female temperance activists could not vote for the laws they hoped to pass. Instead, they used

This 1847 etching depicts the effects of alcoholism. Many women took up the cause of temperance because alcohol so adversely affected their lives. A husband who imbibed could be violent and an economic failure.

petitions and other tactics to get the attention of the legislators.

As more and more women took part in the abolition and temperance movements, they grew increasingly conscious of the inferior place of women in society. In 1837 Angelina Grimke wrote,

I recognize no rights but human rights—I know nothing of men's rights and women's rights. I believe it is woman's right to have a voice in all the laws and regulations by which she is to be governed, whether in Church or State; and that the present arrangements of society on these points are a violation of human rights, a rank usurpation of power.[3]

QUESTIONS AND CHALLENGES

When the United States became independent, it was a nation of farmers. In the early 1800s, however, the economy began a shift toward manufacturing. Harnessing the power of the nation's rivers, mills opened in Paterson, New Jersey; Lowell, Massachusetts; and other northern cities. Young women left the farms to take jobs in the mills, living away from home for the first time.

Life in the cities gave the mill workers a new awareness of the wider world. They labored long hours for little pay, but some began to organize and fight for better working conditions. Frances (Fanny) Wright helped found an early labor organization, the Association for the Protection of Industry and for the Promotion of National Education. Wright was a dedicated abolitionist, and she also worked to improve educational opportunities for women. "Until women assume the place in society which good sense and good feeling alike, assign to them, human improvement must advance but feebly," she wrote in 1836. "If they advance not knowledge, they will perpetuate ignorance. Let women stand where they may in the scale of improvement, their

Troy Female Seminary founder Emma Willard was dedicated to educating girls at a time when few women attended school.

position decides that of the race."4

Emma Hart Willard dedicated her life to the education of girls. In 1821 she opened the Troy Female Seminary in Troy, New York. The seminary was the first school to offer college-level courses to female students. In 1833, Oberlin College in Ohio became the first coeducational college in the country. Oberlin also was the first college to admit both white and African American students.

As a small but growing number of women achieved higher education, they sought to enter professions from which they traditionally had been barred. Elizabeth Blackwell was rejected by two dozen medical schools in 1846 simply because she was a woman. When she finally entered the Geneva Medical College in New York, she learned that she had been accepted as a joke. Nonetheless, Blackwell graduated in 1849 and became the first woman in the United States to earn a medical degree.

LUCY STONE: CHAMPION OF THE RIGHTS OF WOMEN

When Lucy Stone was growing up on a farm in Massachusetts, she noticed that her father tightly controlled the household budget. Her mother could not even keep the money she earned by selling eggs and cheese. The same pattern of male control was true of nearly all the families Lucy knew. As she grew up, she saw endless examples proving that women were not treated as the equals of men according to custom and law.

After graduating from Oberlin College in 1847, Lucy Stone became a lecturer for the Massachusetts Anti-Slavery Society. In 1850, she helped organize the first national women's rights convention, which took place in the town of Worcester, Massachusetts. In the years that followed, she lectured on both abolition and women's rights.

When Lucy Stone married Henry Blackwell, she defied tradition by keeping her maiden name. In the 1850s, she started a movement pushing for women's suffrage based on the argument that there should be no taxation without representation. In 1869, Lucy Stone and Julia Ward Howe founded the American Woman Suffrage Association (AWSA). In 1870, Stone founded a suffragist newspaper, the *Woman's Journal*, which she edited for the rest of her life.

When Lucy Stone graduated from Oberlin College in 1847, she was selected to write a valedictory essay. However, because she was a woman, the college insisted that a male student must read the speech at the commencement ceremony. Stone was so angry that she refused to write an essay at all. This experience strengthened her decision to become a lecturer on abolition and women's rights.

Shortly after graduation, she gave a speech on women's rights at a Congregational church in Gardner, Massachusetts. "I expect to plead not for the slave only," she stated, "but for suffering humanity everywhere. Especially do I mean to plead for the elevation of my sex."[5]

For every woman who managed to take her place in a male-dominated world, countless others continued to live tightly restricted lives. Law and tradition kept them at home, living much as their grandmothers and great-grandmothers had lived before them. Yet change was afoot. Women were beginning to waken to new possibilities.

SELF EVIDENT TRUTH

In the summer of 1846 the state of New York held a constitutional convention. An entirely new state constitution was being drafted. New York citizens had the right to petition the legislature to include articles they felt were important.

During the convention, a farmer named Alpheus Greene presented a petition signed by six women from the present-day town of Clayton in Jefferson County. In part, the petition stated,

> The present government of this state has widely departed from the true democratic principles upon which all just governments must be based, by denying to the female portion of community the right of suffrage and any participation in forming the government and laws under which they live, and to which they are amenable, and by imposing upon them burdens of taxation . . . without admitting them the right of representation.[6]

The 13 colonies had broken with Great Britain over the issue of taxation without representation. Now, six women from rural New York invoked the same principle. Their petition demanded that women be granted suffrage, the right to vote.

These women were not highly educated. They had no history of involvement with abolition, temperance, women's rights, or other reform movements. Nevertheless, they crafted an argument that placed suffrage within the context of the nation's founding documents. Their argument was simple and straightforward. It concluded,

We might adduce arguments both numerous and decisive in support of our position, but believing that a self evident truth is sufficiently plain without argument ... we forbear offering any and respectfully submit it for consideration.[7]

No records survive of the debate over the petition. It did not pass into law, and apparently it was voted down with little fanfare. Several newspapers ran stories about the petition and then let the matter drop. A reporter from the *New York Daily Tribune* turned the story into a joke. He wrote,

What a time for courting, love matches, etc., an election will be when that petition succeeds. It is said to be grounded on the fact that men have managed badly, and that women might do better but could not do worse.[8]

The very fact that a petition for women's suffrage came before the legislature suggests that ordinary women were beginning to share their discontent. Together, they were starting to discuss ways to remedy their situation. A movement for women's rights had taken root and was beginning to send forth shoots.

As women grew more vocal, some men began to protest. If women demanded the same rights that men enjoyed, they argued, disorder would reign and society would be overturned. "Blind to the happiness of their present situation and seized with a revolutionary frenzy, [women] feel themselves highly wronged and oppressed," one critic complained. "They seem ardently to wish for a revolution in their present situation."[9] The essayist and philosopher Orestes Brownson stated bluntly, "We do not believe women ... are fit to have their own head. Without masculine direction or control, she is out of her element and a social anomaly—sometimes a hideous monster."[10]

It was in this climate of hope and resistance, eagerness and opposition, that Lucretia Mott, Elizabeth Cady Stanton, and their friends began to plan a women's rights convention in Seneca Falls.

CHAPTER FOUR

THE CONVENTION TAKES SHAPE

When Lucretia Mott, Elizabeth Cady Stanton, and the other guests at Jane and Richard Hunt's tea party decided to hold a convention on women's rights, they knew they had to plan quickly. James and Lucretia Mott were soon scheduled to leave town. People were more likely to attend the convention if they knew that Lucretia Mott was going to speak. Her reputation could draw a crowd.

Before they said good-bye that afternoon, the women decided to hold a two-day convention on July 19 and 20. They had only ten days during which to prepare, so they set to work at once.

SPREADING THE WORD

Selecting a place to hold the convention was relatively simple. Only one meeting place seemed possible, the Wesleyan Methodist Chapel on the corner of Fall and Mynerse Streets in Seneca Falls. Since it opened in

1843, the chapel had hosted a number of abolitionist meetings. The minister, Saron Phillips, was likely to be sympathetic to the women's cause. As soon as she returned to Seneca Falls after the tea, Elizabeth Cady Stanton visited Phillips and obtained his permission. That night she wrote the following notice:

> WOMAN's RIGHTS CONVENTION.—A Convention to discuss the social, civil, and religious condition and rights of woman, will be held in the Wesleyan Chapel, at Seneca Falls, N.Y., on Wednesday and Thursday, the 19th and 20th of July, current; commencing at 10 o'clock A.M. During the first day the meeting will be exclusively for women, who are earnestly invited to attend. The public generally are invited to be present on the second day, when Lucretia Mott, of Philadelphia, and other ladies and gentlemen, will address the convention.[1]

The following morning, someone (probably Stanton herself) delivered the notice to the office of the *Seneca County Courier.* The paper's editor, Nathan Milliken, ran the notice in the next edition, which appeared on Tuesday, July 11. Newspapers in the neighboring towns picked up the notice and printed it later in the week.

Mary Ann M'Clintock sent a copy of the notice to the abolitionist Frederick Douglass, who lived in

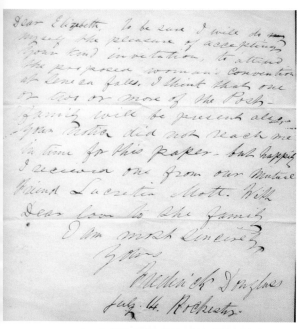

In this letter to Elizabeth M'Clintock, Frederick Douglass accepts an invitation to attend the forthcoming convention at Seneca Falls.

nearby Rochester. Douglass published the announcement in his antislavery newspaper, the *North Star.* Furthermore, he agreed to attend the convention himself. Formerly enslaved, Douglass believed in equal rights for all human beings, regardless of race or gender. In fact, the motto on the masthead of the *North Star* read, "Right is of no sex—truth is of no color—God is the father of us all, and we are all brethren."[2]

Word of the convention spread quickly after the notices appeared. Charlotte Woodward, a nineteen-year-old glove-maker from Seneca Falls, described later how she rushed from house to house with the *Courier* in her hand. She and several of her friends decided they would attend the convention, but only on the first day, when no men would be present.

On July 18, the day before the convention was to begin, Nathan Milliken featured Lucretia Mott

FREDERICK DOUGLASS: FOE OF OPPRESSION

Frederick Douglass (1818–1895) was born into slavery on a plantation in Talbot County, Maryland. When he was 12, his master's wife taught him to read. Reading opened a new world to him, and he realized that literacy could lead him along the path to freedom. In 1838, he escaped to the free state of Pennsylvania, and from there he made his way to New York. Within a few years, he began to speak at abolitionist gatherings about his experiences of slavery. In 1845, he published an autobiography, *Narrative of the Life of Frederick Douglass, An American Slave.*

Douglas was the only African American to attend the Seneca Falls Convention, and his support led to the passage of a resolution calling for women's suffrage. After the Civil War, however, Douglass split with some women's rights leaders, viewing voting rights for African American men as more urgent than suffrage for women of either race.

in a special notice. "Mrs. Mott has a world-wide reputation as a philanthropist and public speaker," he wrote. "We expect to derive much pleasure and profit from her remarks."[3]

THE DECLARATION OF SENTIMENTS

Lucretia Mott was an experienced lecturer, but she had never before tried to organize a convention. Elizabeth Cady Stanton had very little experience with public speaking and none with planning a major event. Mary Ann M'Clintock, however, had organized a number of Quaker meetings and antislavery conventions. She and her two eldest daughters, twenty-seven-year-old Elizabeth and twenty-six-year-old Mary Ann, took leading roles in mapping the logistics of the convention in Seneca Falls.

On Friday, July 14, Elizabeth Cady Stanton wrote a quick note to Elizabeth M'Clintock:

> Rain or shine I intend to spend Sunday with you so we may all together concoct a declaration. I have drawn up one but you may suggest any alterations & improvements for I know it is not as perfect a declaration as should go forth from the first woman's rights convention that has ever assembled. I shall take the ten o'clock train in the morning & return at five in the evening, provided we can accomplish all our business in that time.[4]

On the morning of Sunday, July 16, Elizabeth Cady Stanton boarded the train for Waterloo. Once again, she was welcomed into a gracious parlor, this time in the home of Mary Ann M'Clintock and her family. As James Mott had taken ill, Lucretia Mott and Martha Coffin Wright were unable to attend this gathering. Lucretia Mott sent a letter of apology and promised to see the group on Thursday in Seneca Falls.

The M'Clintocks' tea table was small and round. Built of mahogany, it stood on a central pedestal with spreading feet. As soon as everyone was settled around the table, Stanton spread out her papers. She had been busy writing all week. She

The Declaration of Sentiments was drafted at the M'Clintock home. Located in Waterloo, New York, the Quaker family's house also served as a station on the Underground Railroad.

had drafted an address that Lucretia Mott called her "great speech," which she planned to deliver on the opening day. She had also drafted a document that she called a declaration of women's rights. The revision of this document and the drafting of a series of resolutions occupied most of the meeting.

As a basis for the declaration, the women reviewed and rejected declarations presented by the temperance and antislavery movements. Stanton explained later, "All alike seemed too tame and pacific for the inauguration of a rebellion such as the world had never before seen."[5] At last they decided that the Declaration of Independence, signed in Philadelphia in 1776, had the passion they were seeking. With a few changes, its wording suited their purpose exactly. They called their document the Declaration of Sentiments, taking the title from the founding document of the American Anti-Slavery Society.

The Declaration of Independence listed 18 grievances of the American colonists against the English monarch, King George III. Stanton and the M'Clintocks searched through law books and church documents for abuses of power that could be listed as women's grievances. "After hours of diligent searching, of creeds, codes, customs and constitutions," Stanton recalled, "we were rejoiced to find that we could make out as good a bill of impeachment against our sires and sons as they had against old King George."[6]

M'Clintock and Stanton worked together at the table in this parlor to form their ideas for the upcoming convention. They used the Declaration of Independence as a model for their Declaration of Sentiments.

Overall, the preamble to the Declaration of Sentiments reads exactly like the Declaration of Independence. However, where the Declaration of Independence declared "that all men are created equal," Stanton added the words "and women." "That all men and women are created equal"— these simple words were revolutionary!

THE RADICAL RESOLUTION

In addition to the Declaration of Sentiments, the women composed a series of resolutions to be voted on at the convention. Most of the resolutions called for fairness toward women under the law, and the women felt they would easily be approved. But Elizabeth Cady Stanton knew that resolution nine was going to be controversial. "Resolved," it read, "That it is the duty of the women of this country to secure to themselves their sacred right to the elective franchise."[7]

Resolution nine called upon women to secure the right to vote.

For Elizabeth Cady Stanton, women's right to vote was crucial for any real change to take place. But many of the people closest to her were aghast at her radical stance. "You will turn the proceedings into a farce!" exclaimed Henry Stanton when he learned about resolution nine.[8] He was so upset that he discovered he had to attend to some last-minute business in Albany on the opening day of the convention.

Judge Daniel Cady, Elizabeth's father, rushed to Seneca Falls when he learned that the convention was to take place. According to one story, he was convinced that his daughter had lost her mind.[9]

Even Lucretia Mott, one of the people Stanton most admired, did not support the demand for suffrage. As a Quaker abolitionist, Mott avoided getting involved in politics. For her, the women's rights issue was part of a much broader issue of human rights. Abolition, women's rights, Indian rights, and prison reform all belonged to one movement for creating a better world. If Mott had been able to attend the planning session on July 14, the Declaration of Sentiments and the ninth resolution might have read quite differently.

Despite the opposition of family and friends, Elizabeth Cady Stanton forged ahead. She honed her speech, polished the resolutions, and gathered her courage for the opening day of the women's rights convention.

CHAPTER FIVE

TWO DAYS THAT CHANGED THE WORLD

"**T**he convention will not be so large as it otherwise might be," warned Lucretia Mott, writing to Elizabeth Cady Stanton on July 16, "owing to the busy time with the farmers' harvest."[1] Yet when Stanton approached the Wesleyan Chapel, the streets were crowded with carriages, carts, and people on horseback. People milled around outside the chapel. The chapel doors were locked, and nobody could track down the key. Finally Stanton's 15-year-old nephew, Daniel Eaton, was boosted through a window. He unbolted the door, and the crowd filed inside for the events of the day.

THE WOMEN'S DAY

The first day of the convention had been intended for women only. However, when the chapel doors opened, a number of men and boys made their way

The Seneca Falls Convention was held at the Wesleyan Chapel in Seneca Falls. The remains of the church, pictured above, are on the National Register of Historic Places.

inside, accompanying sisters, mothers, and wives. Lucretia Mott and the other organizers held a quick conference. Expelling every male from the room would be awkward and unpleasant. The women decided to let the male visitors stay, but asked them to listen and remain silent until tomorrow.

By now it was 11 o'clock, and the chapel was growing hot. The convention should have started an hour before. Lucretia Mott called the meeting to order. Mary Ann M'Clintock, the younger, was appointed to serve as secretary. For the next two days she took careful notes, creating a record of the proceedings for generations to come.

Next, Elizabeth Cady Stanton stood before the audience. Pushing aside her fear of public speaking, she explained the purpose of the convention. They were all assembled, she said, to discuss the "social, civil, and religious condition and rights of woman."[2] According to Mary Ann M'Clintock's notes, Lucretia Mott then urged the women present "to throw aside the trammels of education, and not allow their new position to prevent them from joining in the debates of the meeting."[3]

Next, shortly before noon, Stanton read aloud the Declaration of Sentiments. Many in the audience gasped when she read that "all men and women are created equal." The audience listened with close attention as she read the document that she and the M'Clintocks had crafted with such care:

> The history of mankind is a history of repeated injuries and usurpations on the part of man toward woman, having in direct object the establishment of an absolute tyranny over her ... He has never permitted her to exercise her inalienable right to the elective franchise. He has compelled her to submit to laws, in the formation of which she had no voice ... He has made her, if married, in the eye of the law, civilly dead. He has taken from her all right in

Elizabeth Cady Stanton read the Declaration of Sentiments aloud to the attendees gathered in the chapel. Some of the ideas contained in the document were revolutionary for many in the audience, necessitating several more readings and revisions over the course of the convention.

property, even to the wages she earns . . . In
the covenant of marriage, she is compelled to
promise obedience to her husband, he becoming to all intents and purposes, her master . . .
He closes against her all the avenues to wealth
and distinction, which he considers most honorable to himself . . . He has denied her the
facilities for obtaining a thorough education—
all colleges being closed against her . . . He
has endeavored, in every way that he could, to
destroy her confidence in her own powers, to
lessen her self-respect, and to make her willing
to lead a dependent and abject life.

She concluded:

Now, in view of this entire disfranchise-
ment of one-half the people of this country,
their social and religious degradation,—in
view of the unjust laws above mentioned,
and because women do feel themselves
aggrieved, oppressed, and fraudulently
deprived of their most sacred rights, we
insist that they have immediate admission to
all the rights and privileges which belong to
them as citizens of these United States.[4]

With the reading of the Declaration of Sentiments,
most members of the audience realized, for the first
time, that the convention planners were determined

to secure the franchise for women as citizens—the right to vote.

After a second reading of the declaration, several women suggested small changes, which were duly made. Before the break for lunch, Stanton read the eleven resolutions, including resolution nine.

After the midday meal, the convention reassembled for a short afternoon session. The Declaration of Sentiments was read again and another change was made. Then Lucretia Mott read a humorous newspaper article, offering advice to wives. The article was the work of her sister, Martha Coffin Wright. Pregnant with her seventh child, Wright was quiet during most of the convention. Months later, she wrote to her sister Lucretia that she had been depressed in Seneca Falls over "the prospect of having more Wrights than I wanted."[5]

That evening, the chapel opened to men as well as women. Townspeople and farmers poured in to hear the speech by Lucretia Mott that had

THE FIRST CONVENTION

EVER CALLED TO DISCUSS THE

Civil and Political Rights of Women,

SENECA FALLS, N. Y., JULY 19, 20, 1848.

———

WOMAN'S RIGHTS CONVENTION.

———

A Convention to discuss the social, civil, and religious condition and rights of woman will be held in the Wesleyan Chapel, at Seneca Falls, N. Y., on Wednesday and Thursday, the 19th and 20th of July current; commencing at 10 o'clock A. M. During the first day the meeting will be exclusively for women, who are earnestly invited to attend. The public generally are invited to be present on the second day, when Lucretia Mott, of Philadelphia, and other ladies and gentlemen, will address the Convention.*

* This call was published in the *Seneca County Courier*, July 14, 1848, without any signatures. The movers of this Convention, who drafted the call, the declaration and resolutions were Elizabeth Cady Stanton, Lucretia Mott, Martha C. Wright, Mary Ann McClintock, and Jane C. Hunt.

The original Declaration of Sentiments document has been lost, but versions of the declaration have been published.

been announced in the *Courier*. Later the *Courier* reported that Mott spoke by candlelight, eloquently promising "the gradual advancement of the causes of temperance, anti-slavery, peace, etc." She spoke only briefly about the rights of women, concluding that she hoped the movement "would soon assume a grandeur and dignity worthy of its importance."[6]

THE CALL TO ACTION

On the second and final day of the convention, women and men flocked to the Wesleyan Chapel.

THE SPIRIT OF COOPERATION

Some activists in the early days of the women's rights movement opposed any involvement by men. They feared that men would seek to control the movement, keeping women in their place yet again. Lucretia Mott firmly believed that it was important for people to work together, putting differences aside. On the evening of the second day of the Seneca Falls Convention she offered a twelfth resolution. It called upon men and women to work together to secure equality for women in the churches, the trades, and in commerce. Her resolution passed unanimously.

The pews on the main floor filled quickly, and latecomers packed the upstairs gallery. Thirteen-year-old Mary Bascom attended the convention with her parents. More than 30 years later, she remembered "the old chapel with its dusty windows, the gallery on three sides, the wooden benches or pews, and the platform with the desk and communion-table, and the group gathered there; Mrs. Stanton, stout, short, with her merry eye and expression of great good humor; Lucretia Mott, whose presence then as now commanded great respect wherever she might be; Mary Ann M'Clintock, a dignified Quaker matron with four daughters around her, two of whom took an active part in the proceedings."[7]

James Mott, recovered from his illness, was present at the chapel. Ironically, the women decided it would be best to have him preside over the meeting. Even at this convention for women's rights, they felt it best to follow time-honored custom and place a man in charge.

Introduced to the gathering by James Mott, Elizabeth Cady Stanton read the Declaration of Sentiments yet again. After some discussion, Elizabeth M'Clintock and her sister Mary Ann carried the document up and down the aisles, collecting signatures. Of the approximately 300 people who attended the convention, 100 signed the declaration: 68 women and 32 men.

When the convention reconvened after the midday break, each of the 11 resolutions was read aloud, discussed, and voted upon. As Stanton had foreseen, all of the resolutions were easily approved except resolution nine. After considerable debate, it appeared that the resolution might be voted down. Then Frederick Douglass took the floor. "Right is of no sex," he declared in his rich, resonant voice. "Woman is justly entitled to all we claim for man."[8] Resolution nine was approved along with the others. The business of the convention was done. But the work of the women's rights movement had only begun.

CHAPTER SIX

THE MOVEMENT GATHERS FORCE

On July 21, 1848, the *Seneca County Courier* included an article about the women's rights convention that had just taken place. "The attendance was respectable in numbers and highly respectable in character," the reporter stated. "The proceedings were of an interesting nature."[1]

Newspapers throughout the country picked up the story, but not all of the reports were so straightforward or favorable. At first, Elizabeth Cady Stanton was dismayed by the negative reactions. However, she soon concluded that any publicity was better than none at all. "It will start women thinking, and men, too," she wrote to Lucretia Mott, "and when men and women think about a new question, the first step in progress is taken. The great fault of mankind is that it will not think."[2]

WOMEN SPEAK OUT

Newspapers love a good story, and the Seneca Falls Convention provided plenty of copy. An editorial in an Albany paper shouted that women's rights would "prove a monstrous injury to all mankind." "A woman is nobody," screamed the *Philadelphia Public Ledger and Daily Transcript*. "A wife is everything. The ladies of Philadelphia are resolved to maintain their rights as wives, belles, virgins, and mothers."[3] The *New York Herald* published the entire Declaration of Sentiments, jeering that the convention did not go far enough. It failed to demand that women become soldiers and sailors.

Only the *New York Tribune* offered a bit of lukewarm approval. Editor Horace Greeley wrote that the demand for equal political rights was improper. Nevertheless he added, "However mistaken the demand, it is but the assertion of a natural right and as such it must be conceded."[4]

The Seneca Falls Convention did not result in the establishment of an organization to fight for women's rights. However, the leaders of the convention urged that further women's rights conventions take place around the country to increase the momentum of the movement. Early in August 1848, a women's rights convention was held in Rochester, New York, with Lucretia Mott as its main speaker.

In 1850 Lucy Stone and a group of other women's rights advocates planned a national women's rights convention to be held in Worcester, Massachusetts. "We need all the women who are accustomed to speak in public," Stone wrote, "every stick of timber that is sound."[5]

Nine hundred people attended the first National Women's Rights Convention, which took place in Worcester on October 23–24, 1850. Delegates

PAULINA WRIGHT DAVIS: ORGANIZER AND REFORMER

Paulina Wright Davis (1813–1876) helped organize the first national women's rights convention, held in Worcester, Massachusetts, in 1850. She was raised in upstate New York, where she met and was influenced by Susan B. Anthony and Elizabeth Cady Stanton. In 1848, she and her friend Ernestine Rose worked successfully for the passage of New York's Married Women's Property Act. This law allowed women to control their own property after marriage. It served as the model for similar laws passed in other states during the 1850s and 1860s. Davis studied medicine during the 1840s and worked to educate women about human anatomy. After the Civil War, she became an active member of the National Women's Rights Association (NWSA).

Sojourner Truth was a former slave who became well known for her stirring speeches condemning the evils of slavery. She also championed the rights of women. As both a woman and an African American living in a country that afforded rights to neither, hers was a unique and powerful voice.

came from 11 states. With Paulina Wright Davis presiding, the convention approved a series of resolutions aiming to establish women's political and legal equality with men. One resolution called for the civil rights of all women, including those who were enslaved. Among the speakers were Lucretia Mott, Lucy Stone, and the African American abolitionist and women's rights activist Sojourner Truth. The Worcester convention was the first of 10 national women's rights conventions that took place annually until 1860.

Relatively few women were able to attend local and national conventions. Activists used the print media to spread the ideas that grew out of these women's gatherings. A widely circulated pamphlet contained the proceedings of the first Worcester convention. In villages and farmhouses across the country, women read speeches and began to think about their own stifled hopes and dreams. When women in England read the pamphlet, they were inspired to launch a women's rights movement of their own.

Women's newspapers also emerged as a vehicle for the movement. In 1849, a Seneca Falls woman named Amelia Bloomer founded a small newspaper called the *Lily* to promote the cause of temperance, but it soon expanded to include the antislavery and women's rights causes. Its motto was, "Emancipation of Woman from Intemperance, Injustice, Prejudice, and Bigotry."[6] In 1853 Paulina

MANIFESTATIONS DES SUFFRAGETTES A LONDRES

Women in England got their hands on women's rights pamphlets printed in the United States and started a movement of their own. Brave British women demonstrated for the vote and other basic rights.

Wright Davis started the *Una*, a women's rights paper based in Providence, Rhode Island.

Most of the women's rights papers were short-lived, lasting only three or four years. However, they served an important purpose. They brought new ideas into the homes and minds of women. By printing letters that readers submitted, they also gave ordinary women a voice.

AN ALLY FOR THE CAUSE

Though the woman's movement was gathering force, one major figure was notably absent from the annual national conventions. Elizabeth Cady Stanton was at home in Seneca Falls, busy with her growing family—she gave birth to her seventh and last child in 1859. Nevertheless, she remained deeply committed to the movement and was respected as one of its key founders. Each year, she sent a letter to be read at the national convention, although she could not attend in person.

One evening in 1851, Stanton seized a rare opportunity to leave her children and attend an antislavery meeting, where her old friend William Lloyd Garrison was the key speaker. On her way home, she met Amelia Bloomer, who introduced her to a friend who was visiting from Rochester. Bloomer's friend was a young teacher named Susan Brownell Anthony. Stanton was taken with Anthony at once. "There she stood, with her good, earnest face and genial smile ... the perfection of neatness and sobriety," she recalled in her autobiography. "I liked her thoroughly, and why I did not at once invite her home with me to dinner, I do not know."[7] That first encounter became a joke between the two women in later years. Stanton admitted that she did not invite Anthony to her home because she feared that

Women's rights activist Amelia Bloomer became associated with bloomers, the fashion trend viewed by many as scandalous.

her mischievous boys had made the house a shambles while she was out.

Over the next several months, Stanton invited Anthony to stay at her home on her next visit to Seneca Falls. Soon Anthony was a regular guest of the Stanton family. Unmarried and childless, she became a beloved aunt to the Stanton children. To Stanton she was a lifelong friend who came to share her passion for the rights of women. As Susan B. Anthony put it, their friendship was "a most natural union of head and heart."[8]

Before she met Stanton, Anthony was active in the temperance and antislavery movements. She was not inspired to join the women's movement until 1852, when she attended a meeting of the Sons of Temperance in Albany. With several other female attendees, she sat quietly while the men spoke on and on. Finally, Anthony broke with custom and rose to make a comment. "The sisters were not invited here to speak but to listen and learn," declared an authoritative male voice.[9] Anthony stormed out of the meeting, taking most of the female attendees along with her. Susan B. Anthony was destined to become a lifelong champion of women's rights and a leading fighter in the battle for suffrage.

LOYAL WOMEN OF THE NORTH

Stanton was bound to Seneca Falls by the duties of home and family, but Susan B. Anthony had the freedom to travel. She was a tireless organizer, and she carried forward much of the suffrage work that Stanton helped to inspire. When she visited the Stanton household, Anthony often cared for the children, freeing her friend to think and write. Henry Stanton once remarked, "Susan stirs the puddings, Elizabeth stirs up Susan, and Susan stirs up the world."[10]

In the winter of 1861, Anthony and Stanton delivered a series of antislavery lectures in central New York. It was a time of severe tension throughout the nation over the question of abolition. Although slavery in New York had been abolished in 1827, the women still faced hostile audiences. When they lectured in Albany, the situation was so bad that the mayor sat beside them on the stage, a

SOJOURNER TRUTH, TRAVELING PREACHER FOR JUSTICE

The woman who came to be known as Sojourner Truth (1797–1883) was born into slavery in Ulster County, New York. While enslaved, she was called Isabella. In 1826, she escaped from slavery with her infant daughter and settled in New York City.

In 1843, she felt a religious call to change her name to Sojourner Truth and travel the country as a preacher. Although she never learned to read or write, she was a powerful speaker. She spoke out for prison reform, women's rights, and the abolition of slavery. In the years after the Civil War, she worked to help the newly freed African Americans, or freedmen, to find homes and work.

Truth knew many of the leading reformers of her time, including Lucretia Mott, Susan B. Anthony, and Frederick Douglass. She is best known for her speech "Ain't I a Woman?" which she delivered at a women's rights convention in Akron, Ohio, in 1851.

rifle across his lap. He did not agree with their abolition message, but he was determined to protect their freedom of speech.

In April 1861, the tensions that ripped the nation erupted into civil war. Eleven slave-holding states seceded from the Union and established an independent nation, the Confederate States of America. The Civil War was fought to bring the South back into the Union and, ultimately, to end slavery forever.

With the outbreak of war, Stanton and most other leaders believed that the national women's rights conventions should be suspended until the war was over. Stanton felt that women should put the question of suffrage aside and devote their energy to supporting the Union. When the war was over, she insisted, the vote would be their just reward.

Susan B. Anthony was appalled. She was convinced that the movement would lose all the gains it had made if women turned to other concerns. "I am sick at heart but I cannot carry the world against the wish and will of our best friends," she wrote. "All alike say 'Have no conventions at this crisis!' 'Wait until the war excitement abates.'"[11] Six years passed before another national women's rights convention met.

As the men marched off to fight, women stepped out of their homes to run businesses and farms. Many volunteered as nurses in military hospitals. They proved that their efforts were indispensable for the war effort.

On January 1, 1863, President Abraham Lincoln signed the Emancipation Proclamation. The proclamation ended slavery in all of the states that had seceded from the Union. However, slavery

Elizabeth Cady Stanton and Susan B. Anthony put aside their fight for women's suffrage when the Civil War erupted.

persisted in several of the states that remained in the Union: Maryland, Missouri, Kentucky, Delaware, and New Jersey.

In May 1863, Elizabeth Cady Stanton founded the National Woman's Loyal League to press for a Thirteenth Amendment to the US Constitution. The amendment would end slavery everywhere in the United States. Thousands of women went from town to town, knocking on doors and collecting signatures. Eventually, they delivered a petition to Washington. It bore the names of 400,000 women and men.

In April 1865, a peace treaty was signed at Appomattox Courthouse, Virginia. The war was over, and slavery had been abolished forever. At last, women's rights activists could renew their efforts to secure the vote. Surely the time was near for equal rights to become a reality. Yet formidable obstacles lay ahead. In the years after the Civil War, the women's rights movement faced challenges that threatened to tear it apart.

CHAPTER SEVEN

THE LONG ROAD TO SUFFRAGE

"The ballot is the one thing needful, without which rights of testimony and all other rights will be no better than cobwebs," declared Massachusetts Senator Charles Sumner shortly after the close of the Civil War. "To him who has the ballot all other things shall be given—protection, opportunity, education, a homestead."[1] The struggle for the ballot was the focus of energy in the women's rights movement after the Civil War.

The Thirteenth Amendment to the US Constitution put an end to slavery. The Fourteenth Amendment opened the way to full citizenship for African Americans, but it specified that suffrage should only be extended to African American males. Elizabeth Cady Stanton and other women's rights advocates had hoped that women would gain the right to vote when the war was over. Instead, the effort to gain voting rights for formerly enslaved men threatened to push women's rights into the background.

A QUESTION OF PRIORITIES

In May 1866, Susan B. Anthony organized the eleventh National Women's Rights Convention, the first to be held since before the Civil War. When it met in New York City, the convention established a new organization called the American Equal Rights Association (AERA). Mott was elected president. Anthony and Stanton served on the executive board. The goal of the AERA was to work for universal suffrage—that is, voting rights for all, regardless of race or gender.

It was soon clear, however, that most reformers felt that suffrage for African American males was the highest priority. Wendell Phillips, who had been a leader in the antislavery movement, proclaimed that "the Negro's hour" had come. However, he referred to the hour for African American men, not for women of either race.

A few months after the founding of the AERA, Phillips asked Anthony and Stanton to help promote suffrage for African American men. "I would sooner cut off my right hand than ask the ballot for the black man and not for woman," Anthony raged, storming out of the room.[2]

The women's rights movement and the antislavery movement had been close allies even before

A PETITION

FOR

UNIVERSAL SUFFRAGE.

To the Senate and House of Representatives:

The undersigned, Women of the United States, respectfully ask an amendment of the Constitution that shall prohibit the several States from disfranchising any of their citizens on the ground of sex.

In making our demand for Suffrage, we would call your attention to the fact that we represent fifteen million people—one half the entire population of the country—intelligent, virtuous, native-born American citizens; and yet stand outside the pale of political recognition.

The Constitution classes us as "free people," and counts us *whole* persons in the basis of representation; and yet are we governed without our consent, compelled to pay taxes without appeal, and punished for violations of law without choice of judge or juror.

The experience of all ages, the Declarations of the Fathers, the Statute Laws of our own day, and the fearful revolution through which we have just passed, all prove the uncertain tenure of life, liberty and property so long as the ballot—the only weapon of self-protection—is not in the hand of every citizen.

Therefore, as you are now amending the Constitution, and, in harmony with advancing civilization, placing new safeguards round the individual rights of four millions of emancipated slaves, we ask that you extend the right of Suffrage to Woman—the only remaining class of disfranchised citizens—and thus fulfil your Constitutional obligation "to Guarantee to every State in the Union a Republican form of Government."

As all partial application of Republican principles must ever breed a complicated legislation as well as a discontented people, we would pray your Honorable Body, in order to simplify the machinery of government and ensure domestic tranquillity, that you legislate hereafter for persons, citizens, tax-payers, and not for class or caste.

For justice and equality your petitioners will ever pray.

NAMES.	RESIDENCE.
Elizabeth Cady Stanton	New York
Susan B. Anthony	Rochester — N.Y.
Antoinette Brown Blackwell	New York
Lucy Stone	Newark N. Jersey
Joanna S. Morse	48 Livingston. Brooklyn
Ernestine L. Rose	New York.
Harriet E. Eaton	6 West 14th Street N.Y
Catharine C. Wilkeson	83 Clinton Place New York
Elizabeth R. Tilton	Washington Street Brooklyn
	New York
Griffith	New York.

Stanton, Anthony, and others signed a petition for universal suffrage. Presented to the House of Representatives in January 29, 1866, the document called for an amendment to the Constitution that would allow unrestricted voting rights for all male and female citizens.

the Seneca Falls Convention. Now, they competed for the attention of legislators and the loyalty of their own members. To the horror of Anthony and Stanton, the AERA voted to support the Fourteenth Amendment.

Even Frederick Douglass, the abolitionist who had spoken so eloquently for women's suffrage in Seneca Falls, now argued that women must wait. Most women, he pointed out, had the protection of their fathers and husbands. He declared,

> When women, because they are women, are hunted down through the cities of New York and New Orleans; when they are dragged from their houses and hung upon lamp-posts; when their children are torn from their arms, and their brains dashed out upon the pavement; when they are objects of outrage and insult at every turn; then they will have an urgency to obtain the ballot equal to our own.[3]

Many women's suffragists pointed out that African American women would be included if

Despite all the hard work of leaders such as Stanton and Anthony, the women's rights movement seemed to endure setback after setback. Women were still marching for the vote by the turn of the century.

women gained the right to vote, but this argument failed to move Fourteenth Amendment supporters.

In 1867, Anthony and Stanton joined Lucy Stone and her husband in Kansas, where they worked to pass a statewide women's suffrage bill. The bill went down in defeat, but Stanton found a new ally. George Francis Train was a fierce supporter of women's rights. However, he had been a slaveholder in the South, and he insisted that African Americans were inferior to whites. Most women's suffragists wanted nothing to do with Train and his support. "It would be right and wise to accept aid from the devil himself," Stanton argued, "provided he did not tempt us to lower our standard."[4]

Her connection with Train led Stanton to a new claim for women's suffrage, one heavily tainted with elitism and racism. "Think of Patrick and Sambo and Hans and Yung Tung, who do not know the difference between a Monarchy and a Republic . . . making laws for [author] Lydia Maria Child, Lucretia Mott, or [actor] Fanny Kemble," she railed.[5] Her arguments leaned toward the idea that the vote belonged not to all the people, but to an educated elite.

DIVISION AND HEALING

Stanton's racist statements eroded her support within the AERA. After a stormy AERA meeting in 1869, Stanton, Mott, and several other women founded a new organization, the National Woman Suffrage Association (NWSA). The NWSA pledged to work for the passage of a new amendment to the US Constitution. The amendment would guarantee suffrage for women throughout the nation. In response, Lucy Stone and her followers established an organization of their own, the American Woman Suffrage Association (AWSA).

THE NEW DEPARTURE

In 1869, Missouri suffragists Virginia and Francis Minor announced a rationale for women's voting rights that they called the New Departure. According to the Fourteenth Amendment, all persons born in the United States were citizens. Therefore, as US citizens, women had the right to vote already.

Inspired by the New Departure, Susan B. Anthony and more than 100 other women went to the polls for the presidential election of 1872. Many of them cast ballots, but their votes were later discarded by polling officials. In 1875, the US Supreme Court ruled on the New Departure. The justices agreed unanimously that citizenship did not automatically confer the right to vote.

The AWSA did not work for the passage of an amendment to the constitution. Instead, it fought for the passage of women's suffrage laws state by state. The division weakened the movement and discouraged many of its former supporters.

In 1888, the NWSA organized a gala celebration to commemorate the 40th anniversary of the Seneca Falls Convention. It called for an International Council of Women to hold a week-long celebration in Washington, DC. Delegates from 50 women's rights organizations attended, representing eight nations. Of all the women who had organized the Seneca Falls Convention, only Elizabeth Cady Stanton was still alive. Rising to a thunder of applause she declared, "We are assembled here today to celebrate the fortieth anniversary of the first organized demand made by women for the right of suffrage."[6]

Among the delegates who attended the 40th anniversary celebration were Lucy Stone and several other members of the AWSA. For the first time, leaders of the two women's suffrage organizations discussed a merger. Two years later, the NWSA and the AWSA joined to form the National American Woman Suffrage Association (NAWSA). Over Lucy Stone's objections, Elizabeth Cady Stanton was elected president. Stanton's election was largely a symbolic gesture. It acknowledged the importance of the Seneca Falls Convention and the work that Cady Stanton had done in the movement.

When Elizabeth Cady Stanton stepped down as NAWSA president in 1892, she delivered a farewell address entitled "The Solitude of Self." She stated that all persons, both men and women, ultimately must be responsible for themselves alone. They must be able to contribute to society and to survive the unpredictable twists and turns that occur in every life. She concluded,

> When all artificial trammels are removed, and women are recognized as individuals, responsible for their own environments, thoroughly educated for all positions in life they may be called to fill ... they will in a measure be fitted for those hours of solitude that come alike to all.[7]

"The Solitude of Self" is recognized today as the greatest speech of Stanton's long career in the women's movement.

NEW TIMES, NEW TACTICS

In 1900, Harriot Stanton Blatch, Elizabeth Cady Stanton's youngest daughter, returned to the United States after twenty years in Europe. A dedicated suffragist, she was dismayed when she attended her first NAWSA meeting. "Friends, drummed up and harried by the ardent, listlessly heard the same old arguments," she reported. "Unswerving adherence to the cause was held in high esteem, but alas, it was loyalty to a rut worn deep and ever deeper."[8] Women had gained the vote in Colorado, Utah, Wyoming, and Idaho, but the passage of a constitutional amendment seemed no closer than it had been 30 years before. NAWSA continued to hold conventions and circulate petitions, but enthusiasm had flagged.

The dawn of the new century brought a sense of excitement to the nation, and with that excitement came an openness to change. By now thousands of women had earned college degrees. Women worked in dozens of professions that

By the early 1900s, having failed to make substantial progress, women became bolder in their assertions to gain the vote. In 1917, a group of women demonstrated outside the White House to pressure the president directly.

had been closed to them when the Seneca Falls Convention took place. They were doctors, architects, lawyers, scientists, and professors. Some ran businesses, and others worked in the cities among the poor. This new generation of women expected to live and work as equals with men. It seemed only natural that women should be able to vote.

The women's movement of the nineteenth century had been quiet and polite. Stanton, Anthony, Mott, and Stone had held meetings, given lectures, and appealed to logic and a sense of fairness. They were convinced that they must be ladylike if they were to be taken seriously.

In the early years of the twentieth century, women tossed decorum aside. They needed to be seen and heard, to reach people with their message. They demonstrated in the streets, carrying banners and chanting slogans. They rode in hot-air balloons and piloted airplanes, trailing the suffrage message through the skies. One seasoned suffragist, Maude Wood Park, joined a circus parade in Ohio, her car covered with banners and signs. The ringmaster let her give a speech during the show, and the clowns handed her leaflets out to the audience.

During the nineteenth century, most women's rights advocates were members of the white privileged classes. Now, for the first time, the movement embraced women from all stations in life. Women of wealth marched beside factory workers. Interpreters carried the suffrage

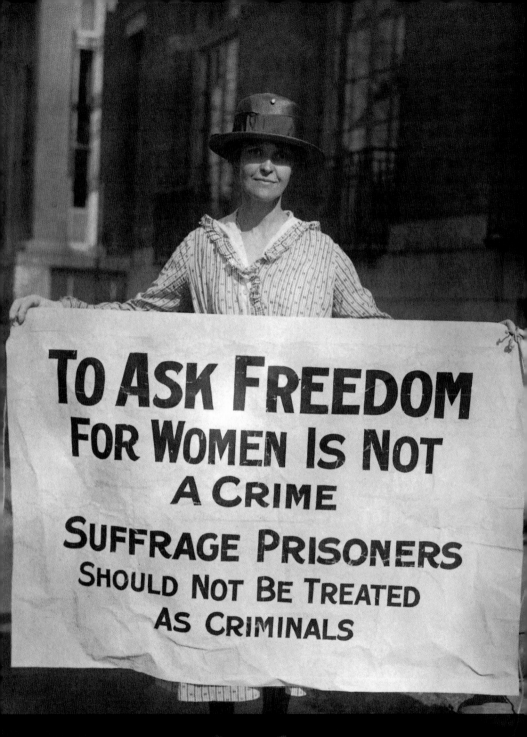

Suffragettes began to be arrested and carted off to jail for expressing their desire for equal rights. This criminalization of the women's movement and the inhumane treatment endured by supporters finally brought about action.

message to Yiddish, Italian, Chinese, and Arabic immigrants. The National Association of Colored Women (NACW) brought a wave of African American women into the movement. No longer did women's rights advocates argue that voting rights belonged to the educated elite. Suffrage was for rich and poor, male and female, regardless of religion or race.

In 1914, two new women's suffrage leaders, Alice Paul and Lucy Burns, founded the Congressional Union for Woman Suffrage (CU), later renamed the National Women's Party (NWP). The NWP worked tirelessly in Washington, visiting lawmakers and urging them to vote for women's suffrage. "For three years every politician in Washington has been followed by a relentless feminine shadow," one woman wrote in 1917.[9] According to one account, New York Congressman Fiorello LaGuardia once told a diligent suffragist, "I'm with you; I'm for it; I'm going to vote for it! Now don't bother me!"[10]

In January 1917, the NWP took a radical step and organized a picket line in front of the White House. Women stood quietly in the cold, holding signs with messages such as, "MR. PRESIDENT! HOW LONG MUST WOMEN WAIT FOR LIBERTY?"[11] For months President Woodrow Wilson remained politely tolerant, and the public grew used to the women's presence.

The mood changed in June, however, when the United States entered World War I. At a time when the government wanted national solidarity, the picketers made a poor impression. The police began making arrests and taking protesters to jail. Each day, more women arrived to fill the places of those who had been carried away.

Once arrested, the protesters were treated as common criminals. They were housed in filthy cells and served food that was crawling with maggots. The police even knocked a wealthy Philadelphia matron to the floor and beat her unconscious.

While women of the NWP made headlines as protesters, members of NAWSA worked to support the war effort. NAWSA president Carrie Chapman Catt expressed her frustration with the NWP and tried to win support through reason and cooperation.

During his state of the union address in 1918, President Wilson gave high praise to the thousands of women who had aided the war effort. "The least tribute we can pay them is to make them the equals of men in political rights," he told Congress and the nation. "They have proved themselves their equals in every field of practical work they have entered."[12] The president stood behind his words. In the following months he pressed Congress to pass a Nineteenth Amendment to the US Constitution, an amendment that would grant the vote to women at last.

CHAPTER EIGHT

WOMEN'S SUFFRAGE AND BEYOND

B y the end of the First World War, suffrage was a reality for women in such far-flung nations as Great Britain, Canada, the Soviet Union, Germany, Finland, and Australia. Yet the United States still lagged behind. After dedicating their lives to the cause, neither Elizabeth Cady Stanton nor Susan B. Anthony lived to see American women go to the polls. At last, with the support of President Woodrow Wilson, the Nineteenth Amendment to the Constitution was presented to Congress.

THE SUSAN B. ANTHONY AMENDMENT

Nicknamed the Susan B. Anthony Amendment, the Nineteenth Amendment stated, "The rights of citizens of the United States shall not be denied or abridged by the United States or by any state on account of sex." In order to pass, the amendment

WOMEN'S SUFFRAGE AROUND THE WORLD

The United States was not the first nation to grant suffrage to women, and it was not the last. Here is a sampling of the world's nations, with the year women gained the right to vote in each.

Australia–1902
Bahrain–2002
Brazil–1934
Canada–1917
Costa Rica–1949
Denmark–1908
Ecuador–1929
Estonia–1918
Finland–1906
France–1944
Germany–1918
Greece–1952
Iceland–1915
Japan–1945
Lichtenstein–1984

Madagascar–1959
Mexico–1947
Nepal–1951
New Zealand–1893
Norway–1907
Philippines–1937
Poland–1918
Russia–1918
Samoa–1990
Sweden–1862
Switzerland–1971
Thailand–1932
United Kingdom–1918
United States–1920
Zambia–1962[1]

needed a two-thirds vote in both the Senate and the House of Representatives.

Some members of Congress remained staunchly opposed to women's suffrage.

Representatives from the southern states did not want to give the vote to African American women; an assortment of state and local laws enacted in the late 1800s had succeeded in denying the vote to most African American men. Women's suffrage might reopen the issue of voting rights for all citizens and overturn white supremacy. Further opposition to the Anthony Amendment came from the liquor industry. Distillers and saloon-keepers feared that women would vote in favor of temperance legislation that would destroy their business.

Nevertheless, some members of Congress had become strong supporters of women's right to vote. One congressman delayed having a doctor set his broken arm in order to cast his vote. Urged by his dying wife, New York representative Frederick Hicks rushed to Washington to vote yes for suffrage. The amendment passed in the House of Representatives by the two-thirds vote it needed. However, it took another year for women's suffrage to obtain a two-thirds vote in the US Senate. Yet the battle was not over. In order to become law, the Anthony Amendment had to be approved, or ratified, by three-fourths of the states, 36 in all.

By the summer of 1920, 35 states had ratified the Nineteenth Amendment. When the amendment came up for a vote in the Tennessee legislature, supporters converged on Nashville, the state capital. The legislature was deeply divided, and no one knew which way the crucial vote would go.

Women gathered around Missouri Governor Frederick Gardner as he signed the resolution ratifying the Nineteenth Amendment in 1919. Missouri became the eleventh state to ratify the "Anthony Amendment."

A single vote in favor of ratification tipped the balance in Tennessee. The critical vote was cast by a 24-year-old lawmaker named Harry Burns. On the morning the vote was taken, Burns received a note from his mother that helped him make up his mind. "Hurrah, and vote for suffrage!" his mother wrote. "Don't forget to be a good boy, and help Mrs. Catt!"[2]

The Nineteenth Amendment to the Constitution became law on August 26, 1920. Seventy-two years had passed since the Seneca Falls Convention passed resolution nine. Now, at last, women throughout the land had the right to participate fully in the nation's democratic government.

Ninety-two-year-old Charlotte Woodward Pierce was the only attendee of the Seneca Falls Convention who lived to see the passage of the Nineteenth Amendment. In 1848, she had carried the *Seneca Falls Courier* from house to house, encouraging her friends to attend the women's rights convention. Now that she was finally eligible to vote, she was too frail and ill to go to the polls. "Now I do not go out any more," she told a reporter. "No, I'm too old—I'm afraid I'll never vote."[3]

THE QUEST FOR EQUAL RIGHTS

"Women in fighting for the vote have shown a passion of earnestness, a persistence, and above all a command of both tactics and strategy, which have amazed our master politicians," declared an editorial in the *New York Times* on August 29, 1920. The editorial predicted, "There will be no solid 'woman vote.' Having individual opinions and preferences, they will be individually swayed by them in respect to any given political issue or personality."[4]

In 1923, women's rights advocates celebrated the 75th anniversary of the Seneca Falls Convention. Women had won the right to vote at last, but still faced serious disadvantages in

THE NOBLE EXPERIMENT

The rise of the women's rights movement was closely linked to the temperance movement, which called for the regulation of alcoholic beverages. The Eighteenth Amendment to the Constitution, prohibiting the manufacture, sale, and transportation of intoxicating liquors within the United States, was ratified on January 16, 1919. Although some women's groups, such as the Women's Christian Temperance Union (WCTU), worked for the passage of the amendment, it was ratified more than a year before women actually gained the right to vote.

Called the Noble Experiment, the Eighteenth Amendment led to the rise of criminal syndicates involved in producing and selling alcoholic beverages illegally. On December 5, 1933, the Twenty-first Amendment repealed the Eighteenth Amendment. The Eighteenth Amendment is the only constitutional amendment ever to be repealed.

the laws and traditions that governed education, employment, marriage, and divorce. At the Seneca Falls anniversary festivities, Alice Paul proposed another amendment to the constitution, an amendment that would ensure equal justice under law for all citizens. Although women had made great strides, Paul and other leaders knew that laws favorable to women could easily be repealed. "We shall not be safe," Paul stated, "until the principle of equal rights is written into the framework of our government."[5] The Equal Rights Amendment, or ERA, was introduced into Congress later that year.

The ERA failed to pass in 1923, but its supporters did not give up. Year after year they introduced the ERA, but each time it failed to win enough votes for passage.

Having finally achieved the right to vote, suffragettes turned out in droves to vote in their first election. Sadly, none of the women who had attended the Seneca Falls Convention were alive or well enough to join them.

THE PERSONAL IS POLITICAL

In 1948 the US Postal Service issued a stamp to commemorate the 100th anniversary of the Seneca Falls Convention. The centennial stamp featured portraits of Elizabeth Cady Stanton, Carrie Chapman Catt, and Lucretia Mott. The stamp bore the title "One Hundred Years of Progress of Women: 1848–1948."

Progress had certainly been made since Stanton and Mott helped to organize the convention in Seneca Falls. Yet in 1948 the options for women in the United States remained far more restricted than those for men. During World War II women had filled the roles of the men who were away, working in factories and handling family businesses. In the years following the war, however, this trend was reversed. Employers gave preference to returning veterans. Women were pushed into lower-paying jobs or edged out of the workforce altogether. Advertisements and magazine articles encouraged women to stay at home, caring for their husbands and families. Magazines promised that a dazzling array of products, such as washing machines, dishwashers, and vacuum cleaners would make women happy.

The lives of middle-class women in the postwar years were not unlike the lives of women a century before. Elizabeth Cady Stanton had thought about "woman's portion as wife, mother, housekeeper,

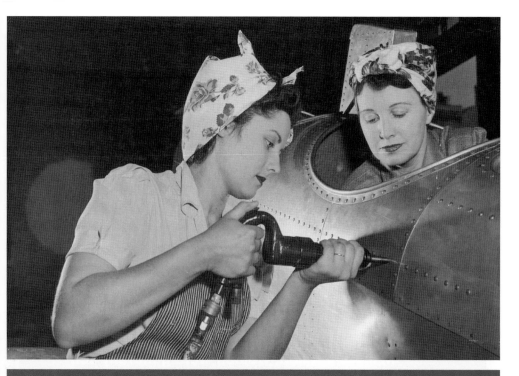

When US men were shipped overseas to serve in World War II, many women stepped in to fill their jobs. When the men returned from war, however, these women found themselves shut out of the workforce.

physician, and spiritual guide," and realized "that some active measures should be taken."[6] Unvoiced, almost fearfully, suburban wives and mothers began to think the same thoughts.

In 1961, President John F. Kennedy appointed a Presidential Commission on the Status of Women to examine the legal and social conditions of women in the United States. The commission reported that women faced unequal treatment at every level of society—in the home, in education,

THE PRESIDENT'S COMMISSION ON THE STATUS OF WOMEN

Shortly after he was elected president, John F. Kennedy asked former First Lady Eleanor Roosevelt to chair the President's Commission on the Status of Women (PCSW). Following Roosevelt's death in 1962, the commission was chaired by Esther Peterson. At that time, a number of labor laws were based on the notion that women were weaker and more fragile than men. These "protective laws" limited the types of jobs women were allowed to hold and required women to work shorter hours than men. As a result, women were generally confined to low-paying clerical jobs.

The commission issued its final report in October 1963. The Peterson Report, as it was known, called for affordable child care, paid maternity leave, and equal employment opportunities. The report helped awaken public awareness about women's opportunities and stirred debate over possible solutions.

and in the workplace. In 1963, journalist Betty Friedan wrote *The Feminine Mystique,* which assailed the idea of the home as women's sphere. The book became an overnight best seller.

The 1960s gave rise to a new women's rights movement that is sometimes called second wave feminism. The term "feminist" was first used by suffragists early in the twentieth century. In the 1960s and 1970s it referred to the quest for women's rights as equals to men.

As the new women's rights movement gained momentum, women gathered in small "consciousness raising" groups to talk about their lives and their concerns. Like Stanton before them, they recognized that their personal frustrations and hardships were part of a much larger picture. They rallied behind the slogan, "The personal is political."

By the late 1960s, the United States was in turmoil. College campuses erupted in protest against a disastrous war in Vietnam. Deadly race riots broke out in more than a hundred cities. Citizens, especially young people, questioned the authority of parents, teachers, and government. In the same vein, women challenged the male power that had shaped their lives for centuries. "In less than two years, [feminism] has grown in numbers and militancy, embracing a wide spectrum of women: housewives, professionals, students, women who are married, single, divorced, with children or childless," stated *Life* magazine in 1969.[7]

Many men, and even some women, felt that feminism threatened the very fabric of society. They argued that women were meant to be gentle, maternal, and supportive of their husbands. Now, all at once, they demanded power in government and in the workforce. They even insisted that husbands do a fair share of the housework and child care.

Yet, the women's movement had become an unstoppable force. New state and local laws required equal pay for equal work. Employers stopped listing "Female Help Wanted" and "Male Help Wanted" classified ads. Battered women's shelters offered women protection from abusive husbands and boyfriends. Increasing numbers of women entered the professions or began to climb the corporate ladder.

In 1972, nearly 50 years after its first introduction by Alice Paul, the ERA gained a two-thirds vote in both the Senate and the House of Representatives. Congress allowed 10 years for the amendment to be ratified by the necessary 38 states, three-fourths of the states in the United States by that time. Women set to work, campaigning across the country for ratification.

Ironically, the strongest opposition to the ERA was led by a woman, a conservative Republican named Phyllis Schlafly. Schlafly declared that feminists were "waging a total assault on the family, on marriage, and on children as the basic unit of society."[8] She founded Stop ERA, an organization that sent anti-ERA canvassers across the country. The Stop ERA campaign

During the turbulent decades of the 1960s and 1970s, a new wave of the women's movement took to the streets, demanding greater equality and the passage of the Equal Rights Amendment.

spread the idea that the amendment would harm women rather than help them. Instead of being cherished and protected by doting husbands, women would be thrust into a harsh world where they could not hope to compete. By 1982, only 35 states had ratified the ERA. Once again, the Equal Rights Amendment went down in defeat.

REMEMBERING SENECA FALLS

At the 50th anniversary commemoration of the Seneca Falls Convention in 1898, Susan B. Anthony stood on the stage behind a round mahogany table. Half a century before, Elizabeth Cady Stanton and the M'Clintocks had sat around that same table, drafting the Declaration of Sentiments. The original copy of the declaration was lost, but the mahogany table stood as a symbol of the famous convention on women's rights. Today, it holds a place of honor at the Smithsonian Institution in Washington, DC.

Elizabeth Cady Stanton and Susan B. Anthony had a deep sense of history. They recognized the importance of the work women had done to uproot the long-standing social structures of inequality between the sexes. In 1880, they set to work on a massive project. With the help of a younger colleague, Matilda Joslyn Gage, they undertook to document the history of the women's movement in the United States.

Not wishing to rely upon their personal memories, Anthony, Gage, and Stanton called upon women across the country to contribute historical material. Their request unleashed a flood of newspaper clippings, legal briefs, meeting minutes, and letters filled with eyewitness accounts. "We stood appalled before the mass of material, growing higher and higher with every mail," Stanton wrote.

"Six weeks of steady labor all day, and often until midnight, made no visible decrease in the pile."[8]

However, some key participants in the women's rights movement did not assist with the project. Lucy Stone was bitter over the division that had torn the women's movement apart in the years after the Civil War. The idea that Gage, Anthony, and Stanton thought they could write a history of the movement filled her with outrage. When they invited her to contribute a biographical sketch of herself, Stone sent back a terse refusal. In closing she wrote, "Yours with ceaseless regret that any wing of suffragists should attempt to write the history of the other."[9]

Covering the years 1776 to 1861, the first volume of the six-volume work *The History of Woman Suffrage* appeared in 1881. The Seneca Falls Convention received extensive coverage, with detailed notes of each session. The resolutions and the Declaration of Sentiments were reprinted in their entirety. The convention was portrayed as the defining moment in a struggle that had slowly gathered force since the American Revolution. The authors concluded, "The brave protests sent out from this Convention touched a responsive chord in the hearts of women all over the country."[10]

If Lucy Stone and other members of the American Woman Suffrage Association had been involved in writing *The History of Woman Suffrage*, the Seneca Falls Convention might have been given less space and importance. More attention could have been devoted to the first national women's rights convention of 1850 and the other national conventions that met before the Civil War. But the voices of Stone and her AWSA colleagues were silent. The Seneca Falls Convention received a place at center stage. In the hearts and minds of America's women, it holds that place to this day.

In 1897, Susan B. Anthony asked Ida Husted Harper, a young suffragist and journalist, to write Anthony's biography. Harper moved into Anthony's house in Rochester, and together the two women sorted through the vast trove of letters and other papers Anthony had collected over the course of more than 50 years. Anthony had saved so many papers that she had an extra attic built onto her house to hold them all.

With Harper writing and Anthony editing, the two women produced *The Life and Work of Susan B. Anthony*. The 1,100-page book appeared in two thick volumes in 1898, just in time for the 50th anniversary of the Seneca Falls Convention. In the same year, Elizabeth Cady Stanton published her memoir, *Eighty Years and More*.

Shortly before her death in 1906, Anthony made a drastic decision. She decided to burn the vast trove of historic papers that she had saved with so much care. With the help of her sister and Ida Harper, she hauled bundles of papers to the furnace and stuffed them in. When the furnace proved too small for the job, the women heaped papers in the backyard and set them ablaze. Neighbors complained that smoke clouded the sky for weeks, and charred bits of paper fluttered onto sidewalks and roofs blocks away. "The task consumed every working hour for almost a month," Harper wrote later.[11]

No one knows why Susan B. Anthony chose to destroy her vast archive of irreplaceable documents. Her actions deprived historians of source materials that would have proved invaluable in future research. Perhaps Susan B. Anthony wanted to make sure that the stories she and Stanton recorded would stand unchallenged forever.

The United Nations declared 1977 the International Women's Year. Around the world, women celebrated their history and achievements and held conventions to map future goals. In the United States, the federal government sponsored the four-day National Women's Conference in Houston, Texas.

Two months before the conference, a group of organizers gathered in Seneca Falls. A descendant of one of the signers of the Declaration of Sentiments lit a torch and passed it to the first of a series of runners. For the next 51 days, a relay of runners carried the torch of Seneca Falls on a 2,600-mile (4,184-kilometer) journey to the convention center in Houston. In a highly emotional ceremony, the final runners handed the torch

THE *PORTRAIT MONUMENT*

To celebrate the passage of the Nineteenth Amendment in 1920, the National Women's Party commissioned sculptor Adelaide Johnson to create a statue of three early leaders of the women's suffrage movement. Johnson's sculpture, *Portrait Monument* represents Lucretia Mott, Elizabeth Cady Stanton, and Susan B. Anthony atop a huge marble base. The statue was unveiled in the Rotunda of the US Capitol in 1921. A week later, however, it was moved to a dank corner of the Capitol's basement next to the restrooms. The inscriptions on the base of the statue were painted over, and the sculpture acquired the undignified nickname "Three Ladies in a Tub."

For decades, women's organizations sought to have the statue returned to the Rotunda. Congress argued that the statue was too heavy for the Rotunda floor (it weighs 7,000 tons) and that it was too ugly to stand among the great men of history. In 1998, *Portrait Monument* was finally returned to its place in the Rotunda, just in time for the 150th anniversary of the Seneca Falls Convention. In 2009, the bronze bust of another leader in the women's rights movement, Sojourner Truth, was unveiled in Emancipation Hall in the Capitol Visitors' Center.

to First Lady Rosalynn Carter, who was flanked by former First Ladies Betty Ford and Lady Bird Johnson.

In 1980, the National Park Service established the Women's Rights National Historical Park on 6.3 acres (2.5 hectares) of land in Seneca Falls and Waterloo, New York. One of Elizabeth Cady Stanton's great-granddaughters donated a collection of books, furniture, and other memorabilia of the great women's rights leader. These items had long been cherished by the Stanton family. Now they belong to everyone.

The Women's Rights National Historical Park includes the Elizabeth Cady Stanton House, the M'Clintock House, and the Richard Hunt House. It also includes a reconstructed version of the Wesleyan Chapel where the Seneca Falls Convention took place. Over the years, the building has served as a movie theater, a car dealership, and a Laundromat. Now, at last, it has been granted the respect it deserves. The Susan B. Anthony House in Rochester is also open to the public. Each year, thousands of visitors from all over the world pay homage to the pioneers who dedicated their lives to securing women's rights.

On July 16, 1998, First Lady Hillary Clinton spoke in Seneca Falls to honor the 150th anniversary of the Seneca Falls Convention. "All men and all women," Clinton said, emphasizing the historic words of the Declaration of Sentiments.

It was the shout heard around the world, and if we listen, we can still hear its echoes today. We can hear it in the voices of women demanding their full civil and political rights anywhere in the world . . . We come together [today] not to hold a convention, but to celebrate those who met here one hundred and fifty years ago, to commemorate how far we have traveled since then, and to challenge ourselves to persevere on the journey that was begun all those many years ago.[12]

CONCLUSION: CREATED EQUAL

In 1848, an editor with the *New York Herald* joked that the women of Seneca Falls had not gone far enough with their demands. He pointed out that they had failed to insist that women serve as soldiers and sailors. One hundred and sixty-five years later, in 2013, US Secretary of Defense Leon Panetta lifted a ban that had prohibited female soldiers from serving in combat. "Today every American can be proud that our military will grow even stronger," stated President Barack Obama, "with our mothers, wives, sisters, and daughters playing a greater role in protecting this country we love."[13]

If he could travel forward in time and hear the Defense Department's announcement, the *New*

York Herald editor would be shocked. Landing in the twenty-first century, he would be amazed to learn that women serve in every branch of the military, accounting for 14 percent of the nation's armed forces. He would see women working in fields that once were exclusively male territory. He

This sculpture, titled *The First Wave*, is displayed at Women's Rights National Historical Park in Seneca Falls, New York. The work features life-size bronze statues of the organizers of the Women's Rights Convention.

would meet female firefighters, police officers, mail carriers, engineers, scientists, doctors, attorneys, and carpenters. He would learn that women earn 60 percent of the nation's college degrees each year, and that women make up 51 percent of the professional workforce.

Although women have entered virtually every occupation, some jobs remain dominated by males, while women are over-represented in others. Men vastly outnumber women in the fields of construction and mechanics, while 90 percent or more of the workers in child care, nursing, home health care, and bookkeeping are women.[14] Female-dominated occupations generally pay less than the occupations in which most workers are male. Even in generally high-paying professions, such as medicine and the law, women's salaries lag behind those of men. About one-third of the lawyers and doctors in the United States are female. Experts estimate that female lawyers earn only 74 cents for every dollar that male lawyers earn. Among doctors, the gap is even greater. Female doctors earn just 60 cents for every dollar earned by male physicians.[15] Women are far less likely than men to achieve corporate leadership roles. Only 15 percent of chief executive officers (CEOs) are women, and women hold only 9 percent of the management positions in information technology.[16]

The salary gap for women of color is even wider than that for white women. In 2013, Asian

American women earned 90 percent of white men's earnings. African American women earned 64 percent of what white men earned, while white women earned 78 percent. Earnings were lowest for women of Hispanic origin, who earned only 54 cents to every dollar earned by a white man.[17]

"Women's choices" are often blamed for women's inequality in the workforce. Women who choose to have children may work part-time or leave the workforce altogether. The lack of afford-able child care plays a key role in these women's decisions. Beyond that is the assumption that caring for children is women's work. Few fathers choose to stay home and care for their children, and few couples succeed in sharing child care evenly. Elizabeth Cady Stanton tended to her children while her husband traveled the country. Meeting today's harried mothers, she would prob-ably feel discouragingly at home.

At the Seneca Falls Convention, a small group of women questioned long-standing traditions and boldly stated that men and women are created equal. The feminists of the twenty-first century carry forward the movement that was launched at the Wesleyan Chapel in 1848. They continue to fight for equal rights in the workplace. They seek to raise the value of homemaking and child care and urge men and women to work as partners in the home. Above all, they endeavor to empower women. They encourage women and girls to hold high expectations for themselves, to recognize their strengths and talents, and to let no barrier stand in their way.

According to an old saying, "A woman's work is never done." A great deal remains undone for the women's movement of the twenty-first century, but women can look back with pride at all they have accomplished since Elizabeth Cady Stanton first read the Declaration of Sentiments at Seneca Falls.

CHAPTER NOTES

INTRODUCTION. "HARD IS THE FORTUNE"

1. *Anthology of American Folk Music.* Retrieved December 5, 2015 (http://theanthologyofamericanfolkmusic.blogspot. com/2009/aa/wagoners-lad-loving-nancy-buell-kazee.html).
2. Christine Stansell, *The Feminist Promise.* (New York: Modern Library, 2010), p. 5.

CHAPTER 1. A TEA PARTY AND A TURNING POINT

1. Carol Faulkner, *Lucretia Mott's Heresy: Abolition and Women's Rights in Nineteenth Century America.* (Philadelphia: University of Pennsylvania Press), p. 130.
2. Ibid., p. 137.
3. Elizabeth Cady Stanton, *Eighty Years and More.* (New York: Source Book Editions, 1970), p. 81.
Available from Digital Library Project, (digital.library.upenn. edu/women/stanton/years/years.html).
4. Ibid., p. 84.
5. Ibid.
6. Ibid.
7. Faulkner, *Lucretia Mott's Heresy,* p. 96.
8. Stanton, *Eighty Years and More,* p. 146.
9. Ibid., pp. 147–148.
10. Judith Wellman, *The Road to Seneca Falls: Elizabeth Cady Stanton and the First Woman's Rights Convention.* (Champaign, IL: University of Illinois Press, 2004), p. 188.

11. Stanton, *Eighty Years and More.* p. 148.

CHAPTER 2. BEGINNING WITH EVE

1. Laurel Thatcher Ulrich, *Good Wives: Image and Reality in the Lives of Women in Northern New England: 1650–1750.* (New York: Vintage, 1991), p. 71.
2. Ibid.
3. Think Exist. Retrieved December 10, 2015 (http://thinkexist.com/quotation/a_woman-a_dog_and_a_walnut_tree-the_more_you_beat/165124.html).
4. Bradford Miller, *Returning to Seneca Falls: The First Woman's Rights Convention and Its Meaning for Men and Women Today.* (Hudson, NY: Lindisfarne Press, 1995), pp. 115–116.
5. Hanover Historical Texts Collection. Retrieved November 8, 2015 (history.hanover.edu/courses/excerpts/195adams-rtl.html).
6. Christine Stansell, *The Feminist Promise* (New York: Modern Library, 2010), p. 11.
7. Virginia Bernhardt and Elizabeth Fox-Genovese, ed. *The Birth of Feminism: The Seneca Falls Woman's Convention of 1848.* (Malden, MA: Blackwell, 2008), p. 2.

CHAPTER 3. THE AGE OF REFORM

1. Valerie C. Cooper, *Word, Like Fire: Maria Stewart, The Bible, and the Rights of African Americans.* (Richmond, VA: University of Virginia Press, 2012), p. 78.

2. Virginia Bernhardt and Elizabeth Fox-Genovese, ed. *The Birth of Feminism: The Seneca Falls Woman's Convention of 1848.* (Malden, MA: Blackwell, 2008), p. 20.

3. Ibid., p. 25.

4. Women History Blog. Retrieved December 14, 2015 (www.womenhistoryblog.com/2012/01/frances-wright.html).

5. Marlene LeGates, *In Their Time: A History of Feminism in Western Society.* (New York: Routledge, 2010), p. 178.

6. Lori Ginzburg, *Untidy Origins: A Story of Women's Rights in Antebellum New York.* (Chapel Hill, NC: University of North Carolina Press, 2005), p. 4.

7. Ibid.

8. Ibid., pp. 8–9.

9. Rosemarie Zagarri, *Revolutionary Backlash: Women and Politics in the Early American Republic.* (Philadelphia: University of Pennsylvania Press, 2007), p. 1.

10. Laura Donnaway, "Women's Rights before the Civil War." Retrieved December 6, 2015 (www.loyno.edu/~history/journal/1984-e/donnaway.htm).

CHAPTER 4. THE CONVENTION TAKES SHAPE

1. Judith Wellman, *The Road to Seneca Falls: Elizabeth Cady Stanton and the First Woman's Rights Convention.* (Champaign, IL: University of Illinois Press, 2004), p. 189.

2. Educational Materials, African American Odyssey. Retrieved December 15, 2015 (www.loc.gov/exhibits/odyssey/educate/north.html).

3. Wellman, *The Road to Seneca Falls,* p. 194.

4. Ibid., p. 190.

5. Ibid., p. 192.

6. Ibid.

7. Virginia Bernhardt and Elizabeth Fox-Genovese, ed. *The Birth of Feminism: The Seneca Falls Woman's Convention of 1848*. (Malden, MA: Blackwell, 2008), p. 84.

8. Wellman, *The Road to Seneca Falls*, p. 193.

9. Bernhardt and Fox-Genovese, *The Birth of Feminism*, p. 10.

CHAPTER 5. TWO DAYS THAT CHANGED THE WORLD

1. Elisabeth Griffith, *In Her Own Right: The Life of Elizabeth Cady Stanton*. (New York: Oxford University Press, 1984), p. 56.

2. Judith Wellman, *The Road to Seneca Falls: Elizabeth Cady Stanton and the First Woman's Rights Convention*. (Champaign, IL: University of Illinois Press, 2004), p. 195.

3. Report of the Woman's Rights Convention Held at Seneca Falls (www.digitalhistory.uh.edu/disp_textbook. cfm?smtid=3&psid=3603).

4. Virginia Bernhardt and Elizabeth Fox-Genovese, ed. *The Birth of Feminism: The Seneca Falls Woman's Convention of 1848*. (Malden, MA: Blackwell, 2008), pp. 86–88.

5. Wellman, *The Road to Seneca Falls*, p. 196.

6. Ibid.

7. Ibid., p. 198.

8. Constance B. Rinder, "Seneca Falls Convention, First Women's Rights Convention." *American History Magazine*, April 1999. Retrieved November 11, 2015 (www.historynet.com/seneca-falls-convention).

CHAPTER 6. THE MOVEMENT GATHERS FORCE

1. Virginia Bernhardt and Elizabeth Fox-Genovese, ed. *The Birth of Feminism: The Seneca Falls Woman's Convention of 1848.* (Malden, MA: Blackwell, 2008), p. 81.
2. Elisabeth Griffith, *In Her Own Right: The Life of Elizabeth Cady Stanton.* (New York: Oxford University Press, 1984), p. 58.
3. Constance B. Rinder, "Seneca Falls Convention, First Women's Rights Convention." *American History Magazine*, April 1999. Retrieved November 11, 2015 (www.historynet.com/seneca-falls-convention).
4. Ibid.
5. Carol Lasser and Marlene Deahl Merrill, eds, *Friends and Sisters: Letters between Lucy Stone and Antoinette Brown Blackwell*, 1846–1893. (Chicago: University of Chicago Press, 1987), pp. 72–73.
6. Edward A. Hinck, "The Lily, 1849–1856: From Temperance to Woman's Rights," in Martha M. Solomon, ed, *A Voice of Their Own: The Woman Suffrage Press, 1840–1910.* (Tuscaloosa, AL: University of Alabama Press, 1991), p. 30.
7. Elizabeth Cady Stanton, *Eighty Years and More.* (New York: Source Book Editions, 1970), p. 163.
8. Ibid.
9. Kathleen Barry, *Susan B. Anthony: A Biography of a Singular Feminist.* (New York: Author House, 2000), p. 70.
10. Ibid., p. 71.
11. Ibid., p. 168.

CHAPTER 7. THE LONG ROAD TO SUFFRAGE

1. Kathleen Barry, *Susan B. Anthony: A Biography of a Singular Feminist.* (New York: Author House, 2000), p. 190.
2. Ibid., p. 198.
3. Tracey Jean Boisseau and Tracy A. Thomas, *Feminist Legal History.* (New York: New York University Press, 2011), p. 143.
4. Geoffrey C. Ward, *Not for Ourselves Alone: The Story of Elizabeth Cady Stanton and Susan B. Anthony; An Illustrated History.* (New York: Alfred A. Knopf, 1999), p. 115.
5. Ellen Carol Dubois and Richard Cándida Smith, *Elizabeth Cady Stanton as Feminist Thinker.* (New York: New York University Press, 2007), p. 128.
6. Lisa Tetrault, *The Myth of Seneca Falls: Memory and the Women's Suffrage Movement, 1848-1898.* (Chapel Hill: University of North Carolina Press, 2014), p. 146.
7. Sue Davis, *The Political Thought of Elizabeth Cady Stanton.* (New York: New York University Press, 2008), p. 216.
8. Christine Stansell, *The Feminist Promise.* (New York: Modern Library, 2010), p. 137.
9. Ibid., p. 170.
10. Ibid.
11. Ibid., p. 171.
12. Ibid.

CHAPTER 8. WOMEN'S SUFFRAGE AND BEYOND

1. Timeline: Women Suffrage and Beyond (http://womensuffrage.org/? page*id* equals 69).

2. Aaron Schutz and Marie G. Sandy, *Collective Action for Social Change: An Introduction to Community Organizing.* (New York: Palgrave/Macmillan, 2011), p. 86.

3. Judith Wellman, *The Road to Seneca Falls: Elizabeth Cady Stanton and the First Woman's Rights Convention.* (Champaign, IL: University of Illinois Press, 2004), p. 232.

4. Modern History Source Book: Passage of the Nineteenth Amendment, 1919–1920 (http://legacy.fordham.edu/halsall/mod/1920womensvote.html).

5. National Constitution Center (http:// http:// constitutioncenter.org/timeline/html/cw08.html).

6. Christine Stansell, *The Feminist Promise.* (New York: Modern Library, 2010), p. 233.

7. Ibid., p. 338.

8. Lisa Tetrault, *The Myth of Seneca Falls.* (Chapel Hill: University of North Carolina Press, 2014), p. 116.

9. Ibid.

10. Ibid, p. 124.

11. Ibid., p. 181.

12. Women of Achievement Library (http://www.thelizlibrary.org/undelete/library/library017.html).

13. "Women in Combat: US Military Officially Lifts Ban on Female Soldiers," US News, *The Guardian*, January 24, 2013. Retrieved on December 30, 2015 (http://www.theguardian.com/world/2013/jan/24/us-military-lifts-ban-women-combat).

14. "Women in Male-Dominated Industries and Occupations: Quick Take." Catalyst Retrieved on December 30, 2015 (http://www.catalyst.org/knowledge/women-male-dominated-industries-and-occupations).

15. Annie-Rose Strasser, "Despite Growing Number of Female Doctors and Lawyers, Pay Still Lags Behind." Retrieved on December 30, 2015 (http://thinkprogress.org/economy/2012/12/05/1284131/women-pay-gap-persists).

16. Judith Warner, "Women's Leadership by the Numbers," Fact Sheet: The Women's Leadership Gap, Center for American Progress. Retrieved on December 30, 2015 (https://www.americanprogress.org/issues/women/report/2014/03/07/85458/fact-sheet-the-womens-leadership-gap).

17. "By the Numbers, A Look at the Gender Pay Gap: AAUW" (http://www.aauworg/2014/09/18/gender-pay-gap).

GLOSSARY

abolitionist—A person who wished to abolish, or put an end to, slavery.

advocate—A person who works actively for a social or political cause.

canvasser—A person who seeks supporters for a candidate or piece of legislation.

chastisement—Punishment intended to improve behaviour.

elitism—A belief in the superiority of one class over others.

enfranchise—To grant the right to vote.

feminism—The belief that women are the equals of men, leading to the quest for equal rights.

freedmen—Formerly enslaved African Americans who were freed after the Civil War.

pacifist—A person who believes that war is morally wrong.

petition—A document calling for political action and signed by supporters.

preamble—An opening statement.

ratify—To approve a treaty or amendment.

resolution—A statement of purpose voted on by delegates at a convention.

suffrage—The right to vote.

temperance—The restricted use of alcoholic beverages.

usurpation—Unfair seizing of power.

FURTHER READING

BOOKS

Boylan, Anne M. *Women's Rights in the United States: A History in Documents*. New York, NY: Oxford University Press, 2016.

Cooper, Ilene. *A Woman in the House (and Senate): How Women Came to the United States Congress, Broke Down Barriers, and Changed the Country*. New York, NY: Abrams, 2014.

Gelletly, LeeAnne. *Origins of the Women's Rights Movement*. Philadelphia, PA: Mason Crest, 2013.

Guilla, Charlotte. *Stories of Women's Suffrage: Votes for Women!* Chicago, IL: Heinemann Raintree, 2015.

Higgins, Nadia Abushanab. *Feminism: Reinventing the F Word*. Minneapolis, MN: Twenty-first Century Books, 2016.

Hoolihan, Kerrie Logan. *Rightfully Ours: How Women Won the Vote (21 Activities)*. Chicago, IL: Chicago Review Press, 2012.

Malaspina, Ann. *Heart on Fire: Susan B. Anthony Votes for President*. Chicago, IL: Albert Whitman & Co., 2014.

Peppas, Lynn. *Women's Suffrage*. New York, NY: Crabtree Publishing Company, 2016.

Pollack, Pamela D. *Who Was Susan B. Anthony?*
New York, NY: Grosset and Dunlap, 2014.

Shea, Nicole. *Elizabeth Cady Stanton in Her Own
Words: Eyewitness to History.* New York, NY:
Gareth Stevens, 2014.

WEBSITES

National Women's History Museum
www.nwhm.org
The National Women's History Museum researches,
collects, and exhibits the contributions of
women to the social, cultural, economic, and
political life of the United States.

Women's History Month
www.womenshistorymonth.gov
Several government resources join together on
this site in paying tribute to the generations of
women whose commitment to nature and the
planet have proven invaluable to society.

Women's Rights National Historical Park
www.nps.gov/wori
Women's Rights National Historical Park tells the
story of the first Women's Rights Convention
held in Seneca Falls, NY, on July 19–20,1848.

INDEX